Anger management

DATE DUE

AUG 1 3 2013			

Anger Management

Other Books in the Current Controversies Series

Anger Management

Lisa Krueger, Book Editor

GREENHAVEN PRESS
A part of Gale, Cengage Learning

NEW ENGLAND INSTITUTE OF TECHNOLOGY
LIBRARY

GALE
CENGAGE Learning˙

Detroit • New York • San Francisco • New Haven, Conn • Waterville, Maine • London

3|09   # 260231120

Christine Nasso, *Publisher*
Elizabeth Des Chenes, *Managing Editor*

© 2009 Greenhaven Press, a part of Gale, Cengage Learning

Gale and Greenhaven Press are registered trademarks used herein under license.

For more information, contact:
Greenhaven Press
27500 Drake Rd.
Farmington Hills, MI 48331-3535
Or you can visit our Internet site at gale.cengage.com

LIBRARY OF CONGRESS CATALOGING-IN-PUBLICATION DATA

Anger management / Lisa Krueger, book editor.
    p. cm. -- (Current controversies)
    Includes bibliographical references and index.
    ISBN 978-0-7377-4130-8 (hardcover)
    ISBN 978-0-7377-4131-5 (pbk.)
    1. Anger. I. Krueger, Lisa.
    BF575.A5A53 2009
    152.4'7--dc22
                                  2008041255

Printed in the United States of America
1 2 3 4 5 6 7 13 12 11 10 09

Contents

Chapter 1: What Is Causing the Growth of the Anger Management Industry?

**No: Anger Management Intervention
Is Not Effective**

Chapter 4: What Techniques and Methods Are Used to Manage Anger?

Foreword

By definition, controversies are "discussions of questions in which opposing opinions clash" (*Webster's Twentieth Century Dictionary Unabridged*). Few would deny that controversies are a pervasive part of the human condition and exist on virtually every level of human enterprise. Controversies transpire between individuals and among groups, within nations and between nations. Controversies supply the grist necessary for progress by providing challenges and challengers to the status quo. They also create atmospheres where strife and warfare can flourish. A world without controversies would be a peaceful world; but it also would be, by and large, static and prosaic

The Series' Purpose

The purpose of the *Current Controversies* series is to explore many of the social, political, and economic controversies dominating the national and international scenes today. Titles selected for inclusion in the series are highly focused and specific. For example, from the larger category of criminal justice, *Current Controversies* deals with specific topics such as police brutality, gun control, white collar crime, and others. The debates in *Current Controversies* also are presented in a useful, timeless fashion. Articles and book excerpts included in each title are selected if they contribute valuable, long-range ideas to the overall debate. And wherever possible, current information is enhanced with historical documents and other relevant materials. Thus, while individual titles are current in focus, every effort is made to ensure that they will not become quickly outdated. Books in the *Current Controversies* series will remain important resources for librarians, teachers, and students for many years.

In addition to keeping the titles focused and specific, great care is taken in the editorial format of each book in the series. Book introductions and chapter prefaces are offered to provide background material for readers. Chapters are organized around several key questions that are answered with diverse opinions representing all points on the political spectrum. Materials in each chapter include opinions in which authors clearly disagree as well as alternative opinions in which authors may agree on a broader issue but disagree on the possible solutions. In this way, the content of each volume in *Current Controversies* mirrors the mosaic of opinions encountered in society. Readers will quickly realize that there are many viable answers to these complex issues. By questioning each author's conclusions, students and casual readers can begin to develop the critical thinking skills so important to evaluating opinionated material.

Current Controversies is also ideal for controlled research. Each anthology in the series is composed of primary sources taken from a wide gamut of informational categories including periodicals, newspapers, books, U.S. and foreign government documents, and the publications of private and public organizations. Readers will find factual support for reports, debates, and research papers covering all areas of important issues. In addition, an annotated table of contents, an index, a book and periodical bibliography, and a list of organizations to contact are included in each book to expedite further research.

Perhaps more than ever before in history, people are confronted with diverse and contradictory information. During the Persian Gulf War, for example, the public was not only treated to minute-to-minute coverage of the war, it was also inundated with critiques of the coverage and countless analyses of the factors motivating U.S. involvement. Being able to sort through the plethora of opinions accompanying today's major issues, and to draw one's own conclusions, can be a complicated and frustrating struggle. It is the editors' hope that *Current Controversies* will help readers with this struggle.

Introduction

> "Diagnosing and treating individuals with dysfunctional anger problems has been an increasing concern to health organizations, clinicians, and society as a whole."

Should dysfunctional anger be listed as a mental health disorder in the *Diagnostic and Statistical Manual of Mental Disorders* (DSM)? According to the American Psychological Association, "Anger is a completely normal, usually healthy, human emotion. But when it gets out of control and turns destructive, it can lead to problems—problems at work, in your personal relationships, and in the overall quality of your life. And it can make you feel as though you're at the mercy of an unpredictable and powerful emotion." Currently, the American Psychiatric Association does not classify dysfunctional anger as a mental disorder in the DSM. Mental health professionals use the DSM to diagnose and treat mental disorders. "Psychiatric patients in the U.S., but also increasingly around the world, receive a DSM diagnosis, and the diagnosis they receive may well determine the kind of treatment they are given, and indeed, in many health care systems, whether they are considered worthy of treatment at all." Ultimately, changes to the DSM affect millions of people throughout the world who suffer from mental disorders. The question of whether or not dysfunctional anger should be included in the DSM has raised controversy.

Because dysfunctional anger is not classified as a mental health disorder in the DSM there are very few available guidelines for how to diagnose and treat angry people. Currently, dysfunctional anger is not viewed as an independent disorder to other mental health disorders such as depression, mania, impulse disorders, and various personality disorders. Those that believe dysfunctional anger should be included in the DSM argue that not recognizing dysfunctional anger as an independent disorder has led to inadequate assessment strategies, lack of diagnostic models to help clinicians understand dysfunctional anger, limited academic literature on dysfunctional anger, and few effective treatments. Also, insurance companies cannot be billed to cover the cost of anger management treatment because dysfunctional anger is not listed in the DSM as a mental disorder. Insurance companies only recognize as billable illnesses and conditions listed in the DSM. Diagnosing and treating individuals with dysfunctional anger problems has been an increasing concern to health organizations, clinicians, and society as a whole. It is believed that classifying dysfunctional anger as a mental health disorder in the DSM would encourage increased research on dysfunctional anger and the development of treatments specific to dysfunctional anger.

Those opposed to including dysfunctional anger as a mental health disorder in the DSM have a variety of concerns. One of their major concerns is that dysfunctional anger may be a symptom of a disorder already listed in the DSM, such as depression, borderline personality disorder, or Intermittent Explosive Disorder. Opponents believe adding dysfunctional anger to the DSM may just be a way for physicians and pharmaceutical companies to label bad behavior such as rudeness, violence, and obsession. It is also believed adding dysfunctional anger to the DSM would reward bad behavior with disability benefits. Another concern raised is how mental health professionals would distinguish dysfunctional anger from functional anger. It is argued that many people are prompted to identify solutions and make changes for the better after becoming angry. The legal community also has a stake in whether or not dysfunctional anger is listed as a mental health disorder. Those in the legal community are concerned that adding dysfunctional anger to the DSM could create a defense for violent criminals. Feminists are especially concerned about dysfunctional anger being added to the DSM as a mental health disorder. Feminists argue that if dysfunctional anger is listed as a mental health disorder in the DSM, violent criminals such as wife and child abusers could use a dysfunctional anger diagnosis wrongfully in court by creating a defense for criminally violent behavior. Also, including dysfunctional anger in the DSM could hold those that display antisocial and aggressive behavior such as road rage less accountable for their actions.

Whether or not dysfunctional anger is recognized in a future DSM as an independent disorder remains to be seen. The next major revision to the DSM is expected to be released in 2012 and will be known as DSM-V. The DSM first appeared in 1952. Eighteen years has passed since the last major revision to the DSM, and many believe that those years have been the most scientifically productive in the history of psychiatry. Health care professionals and scholars around the world anticipate the latest release, which will discuss scientific advances and include research-based information. The viewpoints in *Current Controversies: Anger Management* examines anger management in today's society in the following chapters: What Is Causing the Growth of the Anger Management Industry? Is Anger a Dangerous Emotion? Is Anger Management Intervention Effective? What Techniques and Methods Are Used to Manage Anger? The wide ranges of opinions found in these chapters display the current beliefs regarding anger management.

What Is Causing the Growth of the Anger Management Industry?

Overview: Anger and Anger Management

Jayne M. Blanchard

Jayne M. Blanchard is a writer who has contributed to The Washington Times, Style Magazine, *and Northwest Publications.*

"Anger is an energy," keened singer Johnny Lydon of the '80s post-punk band Public Image Ltd. If anyone knew from anger, it was Mr. Lydon, the former Johnny Rotten, lead singer—and sneerer—in the seminal band the Sex Pistols, a virtuoso of vitriol.

But that was more than two decades ago. Today, Mr. Lydon/Rotten would be better off changing his name to Johnny Flawed-but-Trying-to-Find-Constructive-Ways-to-Channel-My-Unseemly-Emotions. And his record label might force him to attend anger management seminars in order to tap into his gentler, Norah Jones side.

What happened to righteous anger? Why is being ticked off now taboo?

Another emotion—love—has been used to sell everything from antifreeze to sex toys. It is no longer enough to love your spouse, fellow man, or country. You have to express it by buying something. Remember—after September 11, we were instructed to show our love of country by shopping.

With all that money to be made from love—rather scarce in the world last time I checked—just imagine the profit possibilities in anger. Talk about renewable resources—anger is one thing we won't be running out of anytime soon.

An Emerging Industry

Is it any wonder anger has become an industry?

The [2003] movie, "Anger Management" starring Adam Sandler and Jack Nicholson, pokes fun at this anger industry, which, since its inception in the early '90s, has spawned experts, courses, books, videos, workshops, consulting firms, and scores of counselors.

One such authority, George F. Rhoades Jr., has taken a "Chicken Soup of the Soul" approach to rage in his books and seminars. Mr. Rhoades has written separate "Controlling the Volcano Within" manuals for adults, adolescents, Christians, employees, therapists and—perhaps redundantly in our brave new world of psychopharmacology—psychiatric patients.

A Google search for "anger management classes" retrieves 31,000 entries. Anger even has subcatagories. There is road rage. There is desk rage. (Is that when your stapler files an Occupational Safety and Health Administration complaint because you threw it across the room?) There is teen rage, and there is 'tween rage—that's when the alpha girls make life a living hell for the beta girls. You might remember it as junior high school. There is survivor rage—not to be confused with mere survivor guilt—and wage rage.

Anger management has become part of the school curriculum. Such schools as Deerfield Run Elementary in Prince George's County [Maryland] have added the Second Step Program to their roster of reading, writing and 'rithmetic. Second Step, created by the Seattle-based Committee for Children, provides low-cost tools and training to help teach children empathy, impulse control and anger management, according the National Education Association (NEA).

Criminal, traffic and family court judges are increasingly resorting to anger management classes to treat—or, some might say, punish—defendants convicted of road rage, spousal abuse, assault, disturbing the peace and other crimes. In Virginia, the state-mandated courses are offered through the criminal justice system; in Maryland, through the Circuit Court Family Service Programs division. Court-ordered classes also are an alternative to crowded jails and clogged court dockets.

There are no standards for teacher qualifications or curriculum. Anyone can hang out a shingle and call themselves an anger management instructor.

Anger management classes may be just the wake-up call needed for first-time offenders who might have gotten involved in a barroom brawl or taken a swipe at a fellow motorist. But some critics of the anger management movement, like Pamela Hollenhorst, a researcher at University of Wisconsin's Institute for Legal Studies, say that while classes may help some minor offenders, they are ineffective for chronic spousal abusers and hard-core violent criminals.

In 2002, the first person convicted under Maryland's felony animal cruelty law was sentenced. Montgomery County Circuit Court Judge Durke G. Thompson sentenced the offender, Rick Spreight, to jail for 14 months of a suspended three-year sentence and ordered the 21-year-old to receive anger management counseling for beating a puppy to death with his fists.

When Mike Tyson bopped two drivers after his 2001 traffic accident in Maryland, he pleaded no-contest to the criminal charges and was ordered by the judge to take anger management classes. Just imagine—a boxer with anger issues.

Anger management classes are not certified or monitored by state or local agencies. There may be court-approved lists of programs, but there are no standards for teacher qualifications or curriculum. Anyone can hang out a shingle and call themselves an anger management instructor. There are even court-ordered classes available on the Internet.

What Is Anger?

If anger is not an emotion, anymore, then what exactly is it? It is an "issue." How many times have you heard "he has anger issues" or "she needs to deal with her rage before it becomes an issue."

Reclassifying it as an "issue" that can be "managed" detaches it from our emotions, which are by definition spontaneous and involuntary. Such detachment can be useful if you are trying to examine the roots of your fury in an effort to identify and avoid situations that make you pop your cork. But if manipulating language creates a new assumption that our anger is always unjustified and that passivity is the only acceptable response to injustice and evil, then we're asking for trouble.

Would we really have been better off after September 11 if President [George W.] Bush had faced his anger issues instead of smoking the terrorists out of their caves in Afghanistan?

We already have international anger management counseling. It's called the United Nations. But do such infinitely patient sorts as [Swedish diplomat] Hans Blix and [former UN secretary-general] Kofi Annan liberate countries from bloodthirsty despots?

The notion that a human emotion—any human emotion—is inherently and inevitably destructive is naive. There is useful anger—and futile anger. There is justified anger—and unjustified anger. Differentiating between them involves serious and often thorny processes of practical and moral reflection. Condemning anger itself without reference to particular circumstances is intellectually lazy and morally evasive.

Anger must be seen in proper perspective. Like most evolved human traits, after all, it does have its positive uses. In its raw form, anger gives us power and clarity. It sparks creativity and spurs change. Anger can cleanse—and create. It has spawned great literature and art, religion and revolutions.

"It gives us the will and energy to fight for our lives. All senses are heightened, vision is clearer, colors are sharper," says Dr. William Callahan, a California psychiatrist who specializes in anger issues, in a 2002 article in the *Los Angeles Times*. "It has none of the fuzziness that anxiety or stress cause. Anger is a motivator. It wants us to act."

And sometimes individuals—and nations—must act.

The Courts Fuel the Growth of the Anger Management Industry

Kristen Hinman

Kristen Hinman is a staff writer at the Riverfront Times, *an online newspaper serving the St. Louis, Missouri, area.*

In the past three decades, . . . anger management . . . sessions have become a de rigueur punishment doled out by municipal judges.

A touch of schooling and a dash of therapy, the philosophy goes, can treat every little human aberration—for a price.

Pass a check in someone else's name, or siphon ten gallons of gas, and the cost is $65 to $100 for a three-to-six-hour class. Slap a spouse or talk back to a police officer, and the fees range from one to several hundred dollars for an anger management course, also known as "domestic-violence education."

If the class is successfully completed, judges typically reward the guilty with a suspended imposition of sentence, . . . and the conviction is erased from the books. . . .

Growth of Anger Management Industry

Numerous judges order youthful and first-time offenders to anger management . . . programs.

In the process, the judges are fueling a burgeoning cottage industry, one that is "highly competitive, just like anything, selling tires or any other product," notes Mike Smith, president of St. Charles-based Eastern Missouri Alternative Sentencing Services Inc. (EMASS).

Kristen Hinman, "Trick or Treatment," *Riverfront Times*, January 25, 2006. www.riverfronttimes.com/2006-01-25/news/trick-or-treatment/1. Reproduced by permission.

"You come out of the court in Jefferson County," observes one St. Louis criminal defense attorney, "and you've got these service providers coming up to you left and right. They're like drug dealers pushing their products: 'Take my class.' 'Take my class.' It's kind of sick."

Judges control the flow of business, allowing one or several companies to place representatives in their courts and enroll clients after they're sentenced.

Dozens of firms operating offender-education programs throughout Missouri are unregulated. There is no standardized curriculum, no required credentials for the instructors of these quasi-public courses. (One exception: the Missouri Department of Mental Health oversees a class called SATOP, the Substance Abuse Traffic Offender Program, for people with drunk-driving offenses.) . . .

In Missouri, offender-ed instructors run the gamut, from state-licensed counselors to moonlighting secretaries. No one seems to know whether the programs work.

With so few barriers to entry, virtually anyone can start a petty-crime-treatment company.

"I could write a curriculum this afternoon. Anybody could," confirms Jane Browning, executive director of the Washington, D.C.–based International Corrections Community Association, a nonprofit that promotes best-practice policies for criminal rehabilitation programs.

"There's no way that we in this office will ever know about all those programs," adds Ann Wilson, the alcohol and drug abuse coordinator for the Office of State Courts Administrator in Jefferson City [Missouri]. "There's just too many of them, especially in the metro areas."

In essence, judges control the flow of business, allowing one or several companies to place representatives in their courts and enroll clients after they're sentenced. The practice has become so institutionalized that many judges rarely converse with the program directors.

"I couldn't even tell you the names of the companies that are here [in my court]," muses Brentwood Municipal Judge Ron Hill.

What's more, judges say they know little about what takes place during offender-education classes. In fact, one would be hard-pressed to find a judge who has even attended a session.

"I don't know of any judge that has," confirms Judge Ron Brockmeyer, who presides over four St. Louis County municipalities. Judges say they're satisfied, just as long as the treatment companies return to court their participants' class-completion certificates.

"I'm consternated that not a lot of the judges have been to the programs, and they just let the court liaisons come in and do their business there," says former St. Louis Circuit Court Judge Anna Forder.

You pay, go through the motions, get through the end of the class, and go back out doing what you were doing.

Anger Management and Repeat Offenders

Cautions Mike Gunn, Manchester's municipal judge: "State regulation might not necessarily be a good thing. The question is, what do the programs aim to do, and are they successful?"

That's almost impossible to know, since companies don't keep track of repeat offenders.

"That'd be a nice thing to know," allows Alan Carney, clinical director of St. Peters-based Community Services of Missouri Inc.

At a recent three-hour EMASS anger-management seminar in Florissant, the instructor opened by stating: "By attending

25

this class you will satisfy the conditions of the court, but after three hours, if you really do have an anger-management problem, you're not going to leave here with a cure."

Beth Huebner, assistant professor of criminology and criminal justice at the University of Missouri–St. Louis, wholeheartedly agrees. "The programs that work are two to three months or longer." . . .

"I think it's mostly people with drug habits going to these classes to get their sentences reduced," postulates Dave Pudlowski, a former St. Louis County police officer. "And they're no better off than when they walked in the door, because they don't have the psychological problems that the people teaching the classes focus on."

Tyron Henry, a 30-year-old St. Louis man on probation for marijuana possession and assault felonies, reports that he spent hundreds of dollars attending several offender-education programs. He says he got nothing out of it.

"You pay, go through the motions, get through the end of the class, and go back out doing what you were doing," complains Henry, who finally quit drugs and fighting with the help of transcendental meditation.

"If a person makes it two years without a further [probation] violation, that's somewhat of a success," explains Des Peres and Overland Municipal Judge Chuck Billings. "That's the only record we have, because no municipal court tracks anybody beyond the length of their probation."

However, just because a petty criminal doesn't re-offend in the city where the crime was committed doesn't mean he or she is not breaking the law elsewhere. And, judges might never know about it.

Why? Because there is no comprehensive method for searching a defendant's record. Most local judges use the centralized crime database maintained by the Regional Justice Information System (REJIS), but only 39 of St. Louis County's 92 municipalities report information to REJIS. . . .

Lack of Regulation

"There is so much money being wasted on offender-education programs based on schlock science," grumbles one state circuit judge. "It is ri*dicu*lous."

"Every time you turn around," offers St. Louis criminal defense attorney Ed Brown, "the court reps are signing somebody up. You do the math, geez, it's got to be many, many thousands of dollars the companies are making."

Jane Browning of the International Corrections Community Association won't go so far as to call the offender-ed industry a gravy train. "It's better than nothing, I suppose."

None of the five program directors interviewed for this article ventured a guess as to how much their programs earn. They also would not provide course fees, disclose the number of attendees they "treat" in a given year or offer any specifics on the curriculum used.

Con artists . . . [are] right in the midst of the criminal-justice rehabilitation system.

"We license those," maintains Leslie Foran, executive director of the Safety Council of Greater St. Louis. Referring to class syllabi, she adds, "Those materials can't leave the classroom."

Fumes former state judge [Anna C.] Forder: "That is ridiculous! Apparently, they can't even tell you what they're doing."

"This should not be a closed process," says Don Wolff, a former Creve Coeur municipal judge.

The secrecy doesn't surprise long-time St. Louis Circuit Court Judge David Mason.

"They're all lousy," Mason says of offender-education programs. "Did you ask them what their effectiveness rate is? They won't tell you. Ask them how many family members of participants have communicated with them to say, 'Thank you so much, my husband is no longer breaking furniture or beating me up.' They'll probably give you a little line about confidentiality issues: 'We can't disclose that kind of information.'

"Well, hold it now," Mason goes on, thumping his fist against his desk. "If what you're doing is so successful, what's the downside to letting other people know about it?" . . .

St. Louis Circuit Court Judge Philip Heagney puts it this way: "My sense is that people who are con artists, who want to make money whatever the easiest way is, are out there in *all* fields.

"We can pretend they're only advertising in the TV guides or on cable stations, or involved in other kinds of well-known rip-off businesses, but sadly, it doesn't surprise me at all that they're right in the midst of the criminal-justice rehabilitation system." . . .

This is big business, . . . we're talking a couple million dollars [in gross revenues] a year.

Anger Management and Profit

A real hell-raiser during his youthful days in Kirkwood, Alan Carney cleaned up his heroin habit in 1984 and began a career in drug and alcohol counseling. These days, the aging hippie has turned businessman.

"We've got it all," Carney says, introducing Community Services of Missouri Inc. with a breezy, upbeat air. "If you're beating your wife, we've got batterer's intervention. If you're beating your neighbor, we've got anger-management classes. It's Christmastime now, you know, think of all those people that just have to have those little earrings they saw somewhere.

"Well, we've got financial management classes for people stealing. You get a speeding or traffic ticket, and the court will let you come to our driving school in lieu of going to jail. Kids smoking dope, we can handle that, too."

One-stop shopping?

"We try to be," Carney confirms. "We've even got private probation services that a couple of state courts contract from us."

Since becoming Community Services' clinical director in 2003, Carney has helped owner Judy Cowdry double the number of its offices, from seven to fourteen. With so many people to service, they plan to keep building.

This is big business, Carney says. "We're talking a couple million dollars [in gross revenues] a year."

Carney credits Cowdry and her co-owner, Ken Allen, with identifying the niche, but the petty-crime treatment pioneer was actually a Maryland Heights man named Herman Wood. The former social worker and director of St. Louis County's probation and parole services opened Midwest Counseling Service Inc. in December 1974.

"We didn't have to go out and sell the programs," Wood recalls. "We were meeting a need we knew was there."

More than ten years later, Judy Cowdry and Mike Smith were both working as probation and parole officers for the Missouri Department of Corrections. "I had seventeen years in. I was at the top of my pay scale, and I was making twenty-seven thousand dollars a year," says Smith of the moment in the late 1980s when state legislators set about privatizing probation for misdemeanors.

Cowdry and Smith suddenly recognized a business opportunity that could go hand-in-hand with offender education. They left their state jobs and formed their respective companies, Community Services of Missouri and EMASS.

Today, those firms compete primarily with Midwest Counseling Service and the nonprofit Safety Council for business in St. Charles and St. Louis counties and St. Louis City. A handful of other groups specialize in one or two classes.

"We're kind of like the gas station down the street," says Smith from his sunny second-floor office in an old St. Charles house. "We're full-service."

"I frankly never expected it to grow to the level it did," he adds, citing his eight offices in Eastern Missouri and his aspirations of further expansion. "In this business, there will always be issues [for the courts] to deal with."

Increased Workplace Violence Fuels the Growth of the Anger Management Industry

Kevin Quinley

Kevin Quinley is senior vice president of Medmarc Insurance Group in Chantilly, Virginia, and the author of ten books and hundreds of articles.

*A*nger Management is a comedy starring Adam Sandler and Jack Nicholson. In today's workplace, however, there is little that is funny about anger management, which can have lethal consequences.

Workplace stress makes today's job site a pressure cooker that can erupt in violence quickly, often with few warnings. Heightened workplace stress has many causes. Economic competitive pressures, fluctuating workforce demographics, and dysfunctional management and supervision are breeding grounds for workplace violence. People have difficulty compartmentalizing personal worries and keeping them from seeping into their jobs. Company mergers, takeovers, and mid-life career crises produce worker anxiety and hostility. The long-term consequences of such insecurity can be psychological stress and trauma. In turn, this can produce hostility and eruptions of violent or bizarre behavior.

Today's modern workforce often is diverse. Ironically, this creates new pressures. Workplace diversity in ethnicity, cultures, and genders can heighten tension among and within demographic groups. Other sources of workplace violence are domestic issues such as marital problems, alcohol use, and drug abuse.

Violence in the Workplace

Sad examples abound of workplace violence. In July 2003, five people at an aircraft part plant near Meridian, Miss., were shot dead by a man armed with a shotgun and a semiautomatic rifle, who then killed himself. Eight others were injured by the gunman. Surviving co-workers reported that the perpetrator previously had made racist and threatening remarks. Ironically, he just had received anger management counseling on the job.

In Indianapolis in April 2003, a co-worker killed a manager of a Boston Market after the restaurant closed. Allegedly, [manager] Ms. Dickerson had refused the employee's sexual advances. More common, though, are threats, stalking, and harassment at work, often by e-mail.

Companies harbor increasing concerns about domestic violence. Men occasionally transfer domestic violence into the workplace as a way to embarrass and further control women. Domestic violence is the fastest-growing type of workplace mayhem. According to FBI statistics, about 74 percent of battered women are harassed at work.

It makes sound business sense to reduce the potential for workplace violence and avoid litigation.

Workplace violence litigation has increased dramatically. Recent awards include $5.2 million paid to a supervisor who was shot and permanently disabled by a disgruntled ex-employee. A temporary employment agency that failed to screen an employee provided to a client lost a $5.49 million judgment after that employee fatally stabbed a worker at the client-company. The U.S. Postal Service was found liable for $4.25 million stemming from a shooting.

Francescia La Rose, an employee of State Mutual Life Insurance, was shot in the head at her Houston office when her ex-boyfriend entered the reception area where she worked.

Her family sued the firm for negligent security because she had told her employer a restraining order was in place and she feared for her life. The suit settled for $350,000.

Prevention Programs

Effective risk management programs must include strong components for workplace violence prevention. With average out-of-court settlements of $500,000 and an average $3 million jury award, it makes sound business sense to reduce the potential for workplace violence and avoid litigation. How do companies do this?

For starters, an ideal workplace violence risk management program includes common elements:

- Forming an executive committee.

- Assessing current conditions.

- Fixing and implementing policies.

- Establishing confidential information collection and evaluation centers (hotlines).

- Developing training programs.

- Reviewing pre-employment screening practices.

- Reviewing termination and layoff processes,

- Preparing crisis response plans.

- Testing and improving programs on continuing basis.

In self-assessing risk management systems to thwart workplace violence, there are some questions to consider. Do you have a security policy that covers searches, surveillance, weapons and explosives, fighting and threats, trespass, interference with lawful employment, and cooperation in investigations? When did you implement such policies? Do you have a workplace violence risk management plan? This might include work site analyses that begin with a review of safety records, walk-through inspections, and employee surveys or interviews. Is management aware of any areas of increased risk? Such areas might include settings in which employees work alone or in small groups, late at night or early in the morning, in high crime areas. Another situation involves one characterized by any exchange of money with the public.

Implementing employee-training programs can prevent workplace violence, experts say. "Workplace violence is always avoidable," Paul Viollis, senior managing director at Citigate Global Intelligence and Security in New York, told Business Insurance. "It's never spontaneous and is always prompted by unresolved conflict."

Employers must watch for escalating aggressive acts by employees. If trained, co-workers can spot these signposts, such as an employee's making threats to co-workers or damaging property, and report them to . . . violence prevention teams. Often, the people committing these acts give off warning signs. Some experts say that, in almost every case, episodes of workplace violence could have been mitigated before they escalated. To spot precursors, however, employees must know what to look for and how to respond. Employers should not wait for incidents before starting violence prevention programs.

Preventing Negligent Retention

Negligent retention requires proof that the employer became aware, through actual or constructive knowledge, after hiring an individual that the individual was unfit for employment. You may be held liable if you hired someone with a criminal record and failed to know that or, having known, failed to investigate to determine if such an employee posed a risk to co-workers.

Do you check into the backgrounds of all employees as part of the selection and hiring process? What is the extent of such checks?

Consider, too, the nature of the workplace. Courts hold that [some] workplaces, such as bars or similar establishments, are volatile settings that create higher potentials for confrontation. In such instances, a court may impose on employers higher burdens of responsibility.

Workplace violence risk management and prevention also include having systems in place to note or heed any of the following indicators:

Excessive tardiness or absences. Beyond simply missing work, an employee also may reduce workdays by leaving early, departing the work site without authorization, or offering various excuses for abbreviating the workday. This, especially, is an indicator if the behavior occurs in an employee who heretofore had been prompt and reliable.

High-maintenance employees. Typically, employees require less supervision as they become more skilled in their jobs. An employee who has an increased need for supervision or who becomes a high-maintenance employee may be telegraphing a need for help. Managers should be alert to such changes and consider offering professional intervention if the situation warrants.

Work output dips. If a formerly efficient and productive employee exhibits a sudden or sustained drop in work performance, concerns should arise. This is a classic red warning light of employee dissatisfaction. The manager should have met with the employee to identify the problem and to decide on a corrective course of action.

Variable performance. An employee exhibiting inconsistent work habits may need some employer intervention. Usually, employees are consistent in their work habits. If this changes, it can be a sign of trouble.

Trauma from workplace violence is draining enough without overlaying financial liabilities from potential negligence suits. Companies should tune up their safety programs by

adopting these strategies to craft sound risk management prevention policies against workplace violence.

High Schools Are Using Anger Management to Deal with Student Violence

John A. DeMember

John A. DeMember is a high school English teacher in Marlborough, Massachusetts, and a journalist for the Worcester Telegram and Gazette.

Albert Mercado, a Clinton [Mass.] High School guidance counselor, has seen a lot of angry teens over the years.

Recalling one 16-year-old who arrived at Clinton High from Florida a few years ago, he said, "When he got angry, he got angry, and he didn't know how to control it."

Soon after arrival, the student had an altercation in the community. He resisted arrest and faced a charge of assault and battery on a police officer. But after completing a mandated 10-step anger management program, he was successful at Clinton High School and is now in college.

"He learned how to calm down and relax," Mr. Mercado said. "He recognized his triggers." He also learned how to talk to people effectively and appropriately, and how to be a leader.

Schools and Anger Management

Anger management has become a major concern in Massachusetts school systems, according to state and local officials. More than 10,000 students participated in anger management support groups in Massachusetts public schools in the 2003–2004 school year, according to the state Department of Public Health's Essential School Health Program Data Report for that year. The groups provided anger, conflict and violence management support for youths.

John A. DeMember, "Schools Address Teenage Anger," *Telegram.com*, March 5, 2006. Reproduced by permission.

"These groups were only available in 32 percent of districts," the report notes, but there were more students participating in the anger management groups than in any other type of support group, including emotional/psychosocial support groups, which were available in 50.5 percent of school districts.

Districts that do not provide anger management support groups, including Worcester, often use other types of programs to help angry youths and teens.

Anger management self-help groups may be the key to helping adolescents effectively cope with their problems.

Worcester, for example, provides after-school anger management and conflict resolution classes in its secondary schools as an alternative to suspension for less serious aggressive acts and as a requirement for re-entry to school after a suspension for violent behavior, said Judith Thompson, coordinator of counseling psychology and community outreach at Burncoat High School.

Teen Anger

Alison B. Ludden, a professor of adolescent development at the College of the Holy Cross, said there are a number of possible causes for teen anger. She noted that stressful life events that are beyond the teen's control, such as divorce, moving or other major transitions may lead to teen anger issues. Other factors include lack of support, difficulty in school or conflict with loved ones.

"Anger management self-help groups may be the key to helping adolescents effectively cope with their problems and emerging anger," she said.

"I don't think these are easy times to grow up in," Ms. Thompson said. "They have a need to get these skills to cope with their negative emotions in a positive way."

Noting that "anger management is the latest label for social skills training," Ms. Thompson said many youths may not have matured enough to face increasingly complex life obstacles. "All we see in schools are a reflection of society," she said. "Schools are a microcosm. They are public schools, so they reflect the public."

Clinton High School Principal James S. Hastings said the problem is widespread.

"This is something that crosses all ethnic and economic classes," he said, adding that the first defense against anger problems is the teacher.

"At Clinton, we have proactive teachers who have been able to intervene. The teachers see things and pick up on things," he said. "When you know the students and they are having problems, you know how to defuse them."

While only a court can order a student to attend anger management sessions, Mr. Hastings said school administrators can suggest it to parents, who then need to follow through to ensure a child's attendance.

"We have kids in our school that haven't done enough to go to court," he noted. "In the cases I have had, the parents have been on the same page."

A key determinant to a student's success in life is his or her ability to deal with other people.

Often that is because the parents have seen the same behaviors at home, Mr. Hastings said. Gardner High School Principal Michael R. Baldassarre said teaching students how to control anger is an important aspect of education.

"It is more important to teach the students how to get along with one another than to teach them how to read and write," he said.

Indeed, a key determinant to a student's success in life is his or her ability to deal with other people, Mr. Baldassarre said. Those who cannot control their emotions tend to have trouble holding jobs and meeting standards.

Anger and Being Proactive

There is a great deal of focus on both accountability and standardized testing in schools, Mr. Baldassarre explained. As a result of the faculty's intense concentration on curriculum, schools can only react to students' anger, rather than being proactive. But in recent years there has been a drastic increase in what faculty and administrators take seriously, he noted. Violent drawings, threats and rumors that would have previously been overlooked are now investigated.

"The public knowledge (about) Columbine reinforces my increased efforts toward safety," Mr. Baldassarre said. In 1999, two students killed 12 schoolmates and a teacher at Columbine High School in Colorado. The gunmen, Eric Harris, 18, and Dylan Klebold, 17, then apparently killed themselves.

The real danger from anger problems among youth, as the Columbine slayings showed, is that "anger can be much more instantly destructive with guns," noted Francis "Tuck" Amory, a Worcester State College urban studies professor.

Mr. Baldassarre pointed out that students themselves are the first line of defense against potentially violent situations, but a code of silence among high school students can make learning about such potential problems difficult. "Relationships are everything" among teens, he said. It is the principal's job to break the code of silence when it needs to be broken, in the interest of safety.

Masculinity and Anger

Evan P. Graber, director of outpatient services at YOU Inc., a social service agency based in Worcester, said there are many angry kids, but he sees a different reason for their anger.

"There is a crisis in masculinity in our society," he said. "We have ratcheted up the way men and boys need to prove their masculinity."

He added, "We need to look at who is doing the school shootings, battering, road rage and murder suicides—men and boys."

Unrealistic depictions of how a man is supposed to act leads to the ridiculing of school boys who do not live up to that image, Mr. Graber said.

"A lot of these school shootings were done by kids that felt that they were picked on and were exacting revenge," he said. "There is an assumption that there is only one way to be a man. God forbid if a boy is into poetry or theater."

Slang phrases with implicit messages such as "Tough it out," or "Suck it up," create an emotional disconnect within males, he said. "There are multiple ways to being a man," he said, and young people need to know that.

"Until it becomes important to men, collectively, we have a real problem in society," Mr. Graber concluded.

Anger Management Trend

Mr. Amory, who has been a licensed social worker for more than 30 years in addition to teaching at Worcester State, acknowledged that there are many angry high school students, but suggested that anger management programs may be just the latest trend for dealing with behavior problems.

"Anger management might be the new fad, like Hula-Hoops, or it could really help," he said.

He noted that there is a financial incentive for schools to buy into the anger management trend.

"Essentially, the school gets paid a certain amount for every kid they have—and for every special ed kid, they receive considerably more," he explained. "It was the same thing with attention deficit disorder. They were throwing Ritalin at everyone, even ones who clearly didn't benefit from it."

And there is yet another potential negative aspect to the anger management trend, according to Mr. Amory. When not managed appropriately, anger management classes can create a stigma for a student that is counterproductive.

"It can ultimately result in the labeling of kids as bad and deviant, and the teachers may avoid the student due to this label," he said.

Claire T. Russell, director of children's outpatient services at Community Healthlink of Worcester, said she believes that some young people who seem angry are not angry at all.

"When kids are overstressed, their behavior may be seen as anger," she said. "Assessment is so critical."

Mr. Graber, of YOU Inc., agreed that stress can lead to bad behavior.

"The pressures of school achievement, sports and over-scheduling put a lot of stress on kids, and one way the stress comes out is frustration and anger," he said.

Women's Success Fuels the Growth of the Anger Management Industry

Emma Cowing

Emma Cowing is a senior writer for The Scotsman, *Scotland's national newspaper.*

As the news filtered through, late on Wednesday night, that the supermodel Naomi Campbell had been arrested for an alleged assault on a woman thought to be her counsellor, a million heads were shaken in disbelief. Surely she hadn't flown off the handle again?

If she did, she is not alone. We've seen a string of female celebrities let rip in public, including the usually enigmatic Madonna, who raged against the media's reaction to her adoption of an African baby boy on *The Oprah Winfrey Show*, and Heather Mills, who seems intent on waging a terrifying revenge on her estranged husband, Paul McCartney, accusing him of verbal and physical abuse as the couple draw the battle lines in what promises to be a bitter divorce.

And they're not the only high-profile women raging against the machine, their fans, or even their loved ones. There's Courtney Love, who has had a string of assault charges filed against her and once hit a fan over the head with a microphone stand; Sienna Miller, whose tirades against the paparazzi and public arguments with on-off boyfriend Jude Law are notorious; Jennifer Lopez, who has a reputation for outrageous diva demands; even the odious Nikki Grahame, a runner-up in this year's *Big Brother* series, who appears to have built an entire career around being a stroppy, screamy, argumentative little madam. Forget the Chinese year of the dog—so far 2006 is shaping up to be the year of the angry woman.

Women and Anger

But are these raging celebrities merely the exceptions that prove the rule? Or are women really getting angrier? According to Mike Fisher, director of the British Association of Anger Management (BAAM), there has been a marked increase in recent years in the number of women seeking help with their anger issues.

"Over the past seven years or so the split between men and women coming to anger-management classes has been 60/40," he says. "However, over the past year and a half that's narrowed to 55/45. We're certainly seeing more women."

And according to Mr Fisher, the reason more women are getting angrier is a reflection of increasing success in all areas of their life.

"As women become more empowered and take their rightful place in society as equal partners to men, they become equal decision makers," says Fisher. "Unfortunately, having to be assertive in that decision-making process can mean that they become aggressive."

A survey conducted [in 2005] by BAAM concluded that women are far more likely than men to be angry at home—venting their spleen in the privacy of their own four walls. The men, meanwhile, are more likely to get angry in the workplace.

"Women face a lot of sexism in the workplace and the stress they're under means they will take issues from their work home with them," says Mr Fisher.

"They'll stuff their emotions back down when they're at work and then when they get home, drop hand grenades that affect their partner and their children."

Thanks to ever-busier lives filled with work, children, responsibilities at home and at the office—not to mention the responsibility to look good all the time—it's no wonder that sometimes the pressure becomes unbearable. This can increasingly happen when strong emotions have been suppressed, a bad habit to which women are particularly prone.

Recent research from the University of Aberdeen shows that women who suppress their emotions can be left with even more angry feelings—and certainly more than men. The survey used interviews of more than 20,000 people born in 1958 and 1970, tracking responses through adulthood, and found that women were more likely to report "persistent anger" by a small but significant margin.

No wonder, then, that in August of [2006], a woman ran over two others in her Jeep after they cut in front of her in the queue at a McDonald's in Georgia, USA. Or that Jeanine Pirro, once seen as a rising star of women's Republican politics and a challenger to Hillary Clinton in the US Senate, lost her rag with her husband, whom she suspected of infidelity, then had him followed, and is now under government investigation for being what she describes as "a very angry woman".

Types of Anger

There are, of course, says Mr Fisher, different types of anger, and Naomi Campbell's particular propensity is, he believes, a result of her privileged and high-profile life.

"Naomi Campbell is what we would call a 'high-chair tyrant'," he says. "Successful at 15, the first black model in Vogue, worth millions of pounds—she's in the sort of position where other people jump to do what she wants. That means she feels she can act without consequences and that she takes things personally that she really shouldn't."

Campbell has attended anger-management classes before and it is ironic that it was against her counsellor that this latest alleged attack took place. So, can anger management really work for women?

"First, women need to identify their needs," says Mr Fisher. "They need to feel valued and understood and cared for, as though they are trusted and that they belong. But they also need to articulate that to those who need to know it.

"They also need to work on developing communication skills that won't cause confrontation and conflict."

Mr Fisher also blames anger on low self-esteem, something that could easily be attributed to the daily onslaught each woman receives thanks to the endless images in the media of beautiful models and celebrities.

Perhaps, then, seeing the likes of Naomi, Madonna et al go postal in public assures women in general, if nothing else, that perhaps being angry is reasonably normal.

And while no one will condone physical violence of the kind that Campbell is alleged to have carried out, it is worth bearing in mind that if women hadn't got angry in the first place, the feminist revolution may never have happened.

As veteran women's activist Sheila Jeffreys once said: "You have to be enraged. Rage is absolutely fundamental—not anger, it's not strong enough. It has to be rage."

But it is better done within acceptable boundaries.

CHAPTER 2

Is Anger a Dangerous Emotion?

Chapter Preface

Anger is a natural human emotion that can result in either positive or negative outcomes. It is not just experienced by individuals; it can also be experienced by groups of people. When a group of people becomes angry regarding a particular issue, they often ban together to express their beliefs, resulting in social anger. Examples of social anger include the women's suffrage movement, the Los Angeles Riots of 1992, and the unifying of America after the 9/11 attacks. In the past, social anger has resulted in positive societal change as well as dangerous incidents.

The women's suffrage movement is a direct result of women around the world becoming angry and *demanding* change. Social psychologist Carol Tavris, author of *Anger: The Misunderstood Emotion* asks her readers to consider another, nonangry scenario, "Imagine what the women's suffrage movement would have been like if women had [merely] said, 'Guys, it's really so unfair, we're nice people and we're human beings too. Won't you listen to us and give us the vote?" Anger has not only resulted in women having the right to vote but has also given women the opportunity to make reproductive decisions and has created workplace rights for women regarding maternity leave, sexual harassment, and pay discrimination.

The Los Angeles Riots of 1992 were a direct result of the anger experienced by the black community following the Rodney King verdict. On April 29, 1992, a jury acquitted four Los Angeles police officers for beating African American Rodney King following a high-speed pursuit. Prior to the verdict a recording of the incident was played repeatedly in the media. The recording clearly showed King being beaten by the officers. The officers involved claimed the recording failed to show King's resisting of arrest. The Rodney King verdict led to mass riots in the streets of Los Angeles lasting for more than six days. It is believed the riots were not only a result of the Rodney King verdict but also of suppressed anger felt by the black community due to high unemployment and the Los Angeles police department's previous racial discrimination. The riot resulted in a retrial of the four officers charged with federal civil rights violations. The outcome of the retrial resulted in two officers being found guilty and two acquitted.

After the 9/11 attacks the anger experienced by America unified the congressional parties. CNN reported on Sept 12, 2001, "Members of Congress promised to "stand together" and vowed revenge in the aftermath of terror attacks Tuesday that killed hundreds, perhaps thousands, in Washington and New York." When visiting the World Trade Center site following the attacks, President George W. Bush expressed his anger by stating to a cheering crowd, "I can hear you. The rest of the world hears you. The people who knocked down this building will hear all of us soon." This public outrage put pressure on the president and Congress to take unified action: On October 7, 2001, the war on terror began in Afghanistan.

The viewpoints in the following chapters examine both the dangerous and positive aspects of anger in people's personal lives.

Suppressed Anger Leads to Health Problems

Dorothy Foltz-Gray

Dorothy Foltz-Gray is a past recipient of the Tennessee Arts Commission's Individual Artist's Fellowship and the Poetry Society of America's Award for Narrative Poetry.

When Pat Willard was 6, her older cousins wouldn't let her join in their game. She pitched a fit, and someone snapped a photo of the moment: She's screaming—face flushed, eyes closed—and her father has his arms and legs wrapped around her, holding her so she won't hurt herself. "I was this little spitfire with an Irish temper," says Willard, now 47, and director of communications at the City University of New York. "But tantrums didn't fit well with the good-girl thing. They were not genteel." Instead, her mother's silent fury became her model for anger. When her mom got mad, she turned dead quiet, not speaking for days. "She would not say why she was angry," says Willard. "But the house got black."

So Willard learned, as countless women have, to hide her temper. By the time she was in her 30s, she had high blood pressure, headaches, rashes, depression, difficulty parenting two young sons, and a troubled marriage. But it never occurred to her to think of herself as angry. Rather, she thought she was a bad mom and a stifled wife. Depression, not anger, was the red flag that hustled her into therapy.

Willard's story isn't unusual: Many women, unlike most men, tend to express their anger indirectly, research finds, and the result can be depression, heart disease, or an earlier death, regardless of the cause. Unfortunately, blowing up has health consequences as well. So what's a pissed-off woman to do? If you learn to release hostility in a controlled and constructive manner, you will add years—and satisfaction—to your life.

Quashing Emotion

Why do women struggle with anger? Many learned to bury feelings from their mothers and grandmothers, whose silences protected marriages that were their livelihoods. They couldn't risk behavior that might get them booted out of the house. As Willard's mother believed, anger turned you into a fishmonger screaming in the streets.

"Feeling the emotion meant they'd be tempted to show it," says Deborah L. Cox, PhD, an associate professor of counseling at Missouri State University and coauthor of *The Anger Advantage*. Many simply stopped experiencing anger as anger: It became depression or frustration, emotions safer to express.

Although younger women may believe they're comfortable being assertive, when it comes to anger, they still struggle, says psychologist Sandra Thomas, PhD, chair of the PhD program in nursing at the University of Tennessee, where she has been studying women and anger for 15 years. "A college woman, for example, may be freer with profanity, but she is still reluctant to tell her boyfriend she's angry if she thinks an outburst will drive him away," says Thomas.

Studies [link] suppressed anger to cardiac problems, high blood pressure, headaches, irritable bowel syndrome, and cancer.

Paying Anger's Price

But hiding anger may be far more costly than losing a relationship: A [2005] study by Cox and others revealed that women who deal with anger indirectly or attempt to suppress it are—as Willard was—more likely to experience depression, anxiety, and physical complaints than women who are more direct.

Such suppression may even be deadly. [In February 2005], Wisconsin epidemiologist Elaine D. Eaker, ScD, and colleagues from Boston University announced the findings of a decade-long study of 1,500 married women. Those who suppressed feelings of any kind—anger, depression, frustration—during conflicts with their spouses were four times more likely to die of all causes during the 10-year follow-up than those who spoke up. "Being quiet may or may not protect your marriage," says Eaker, "but you sure aren't doing your health any good by being silent."

Eaker's research comes on the heels of other studies linking suppressed anger to cardiac problems, high blood pressure, headaches, irritable bowel syndrome, and cancer. In a notable study from 2003, researchers at Columbia University did emotional screenings on more than 300 middle-aged women with coronary heart disease: 50% were angry and 37% were depressed.

Women choking back fury are often the ones tossing and turning at night, as well, ruminating over what they wish they'd said during an incident, stoking the internal fires. "Anger is an energy," says Thomas. "If it's not expressed, your heart rate and blood pressure rise; your stomach acids churn." Anger triggers a fight-or-flight reaction: Adrenaline and other stress hormones rise, breathing rate increases, and muscles tighten. Your body revs up, and when anger is chronic, it stays revved.

Finding Hidden Rage

"Anger's shadows are everywhere," says Cox. "If you don't think you are angry, look at other parts of your life." Do you eat or drink too much and then regret it? Are you a perfectionist who has to be on top of things, who has no other life but looking perfect, being just-right thin, and working hard without ever relaxing? And how's your sex life? Is sex painful?

A 2002 study by Sally Stabb, PhD, an associate professor of counseling psychology at Texas Woman's University and co-author with Cox of *The Anger Advantage*, found that women who repress their anger have more critical feelings about their bodies and more negative physical experiences—like pain—during sex.

But the biggest clue to hidden anger in women is often depression, says psychologist Dana Jack, EdD, a professor of interdisciplinary studies at Fairhaven College/Western Washington University and author of *Behind the Mask: Destruction and Creativity in Women's Aggression*, "If a woman is unaware of her anger or thinks it's bad, she can float from anger straight to depression," Jack says. "I often suggest to women that every time they see their mood collapse, they chart what happened just before, and it's usually that they got angry. But we feel like we're forbidden to feel that, so instead we get depressed."

Suppressing Anger

Even if you blow up from time to time, you can't assume that you're not a suppressor. Cox and her colleagues divide suppressors into four types:

1. *Container.* She knows she's angry but chooses to hold it in and hopes it will blow over. Most of us are containers at least some of the time.

2. *Internalizer.* She blames herself for whatever happens to her, absorbing the anger she really feels about other people. She's often full of self-loathing.

3. *Segmenter.* She denies her anger in part because she finds it an ugly trait. She tends to be passive-aggressive, another way women reroute or disguise anger, says Jack. "For example, you say you'll do something and then not do it. Or you may switch targets, feeling fury at your husband but getting mad at your kids instead." This is

the type that most alarms Cox, who notes, "If you don't even realize you're angry, it's very difficult to do something about it."

4. *Externalizer.* She contains her anger until she simply explodes, usually at people who are less powerful than she is. "Some women swing from silence to aggressive anger," says Jack. "But just acting out doesn't help. That creates guilt and shame and reinforces the notion that anger is bad." Actually, this aggressive, explosive anger— throwing things, screaming—usually causes more frustration, says Jack. "It's indirect because you're not talking about the problem that caused the anger. And exploding can make a woman feel more powerless because it rarely changes anything." In Cox's study, externalizers had the most physical symptoms, including headaches, stomach problems, and upper respiratory infections.

"But there is no one pure type," says Thomas. "You may be a woman who explodes at home but never at work. Or one who could never show anger to your mother but can to your kids." Parks, for example, always saw herself as someone who had difficulty hiding her emotions. "If I'm upset, it's evident," she says.

Yet she wrapped anger in sarcastic comments that never improved her relationships with others. Another muffle: turning the anger against yourself. "You're a safe target," says Jack.

Writing about your anger helps you acknowledge and begin to understand it.

Releasing the Beast

Aiding us in all this subterfuge is confusion about anger itself. "Many women think anger is a bad thing, and if they are angry, something is wrong with them," says psychiatrist Jean Baker Miller, MD, director of the Jean Baker Miller Training Institute at the Stone Center in Wellesley, MA, where she researches women and anger. "But anger is an emotional reaction indicating that something is wrong and that something needs to be done."

In fact, women's anger usually centers on their most intimate relationships—their husbands, their mothers, their best friends, says Thomas, who has interviewed both men and women extensively about their anger. "Anger for women is intermingled with hurt and pain because they cannot understand how a person they are close to could behave a certain way. We never, ever interviewed a woman who didn't mention her partner. Never." Yet men tend to focus on other parts of their lives, like cars and politics, she says. They tell stories of vehicles that are lemons, or computers that don't work, or politicians who are louses.

A woman's focus on intimate relationships may also increase her vulnerability to anger's ravages. According to Timothy W. Smith, PhD, a psychologist studying anger, marriage, and heart health at the University of Utah, angry women married to angry husbands face a twofold hit. He's found that not only does their own anger raise heart rate and blood pressure, but their angry spouses also up their stress, increasing heart risk even more. . . .

Embracing Fury

Examine your anger roots. You can't learn to express anger until you know how you experience it now and where that style originated. Ask yourself how your parents got angry. Were you allowed to lose your temper, or were you punished for it? Once Willard understood that her own silence, ill health, and relationship woes were the legacy of her mother's anger, it also became clearer what patterns she had to break. "I had to learn to say how I felt," she says.

Try a practice session. If you're a suppressor, chances are that expressing your anger feels pretty awkward. Jack suggests practicing with friends before you speak with the person you're mad at.

Share the anger. Talk about the anger you feel, with the goal of solving a specific problem. If you're angry with your spouse or someone close to you, talk calmly with that person about your pattern of anger. "Look at how anger works in your relationship," says Jack. "If you have a husband who is going to escalate the anger, tell him that his anger silences you, that you can't communicate your feelings because you know he'll go ballistic."

Willard would get so angry that she couldn't speak. "But my husband, who had gone into therapy, too, helped me find a vocabulary," she says. "He would sit down with me and say, 'Let's go through the situation.' We started going back and forth about the words, talking about how you share your displeasure."

Put pen to paper. Writing about your anger helps you acknowledge and begin to understand it, says James W. Pennebaker, PhD, a professor of psychology at the University of Texas. "Ask yourself in writing what makes you angry in a certain situation or person. That process helps undermine the anger both psychologically and physiologically." Thomas also suggests that women keep a journal, reflecting on incidents they feel angry about. "Women often get confused during an angry episode because it's so distressing and they find themselves thinking afterward, What started that? But if you keep a record for a month of angry incidents with a specific person, for example, you will begin to see recurring themes. Once you've calmed down, you can talk to that person about the anger in a clearer way."

Managing the Argument

Calm your body. "If you're aware you're angry, stop and ask, What do I need to do about this?" advises Stabb. "Taking time to calm down is important because it gives you time to process the information your emotions are telling you."

Stick to specifics. Instead of beginning by hurling accusations and cries of "You always do this," talk only about the specific incident that angered you, suggests Thomas. "Let's say your husband is 45 minutes late to meet you. Begin by saying, 'We were supposed to meet at 7 and you came at 7:45. I'm really angry and I want to talk to you about this.' Then state a consequence: 'Next time, I won't wait.' State the anger clearly and make sure you follow through."

Learn to listen. Part of processing anger is being able to listen to another person's feelings as well as expressing your own, says Stabb. "You can acknowledge his anger without agreeing by saying something like, 'I know that you have a different point of view from mine, but this is my point of view and this is why I feel angry.'" Acknowledging another's anger makes it more likely he'll accept yours.

As [she] found words for her anger, her depression lifted, her health problems abated, her self-esteem rose, and her marriage righted itself.

Take an anger break. Don't expect to overhaul a situation or your anger all at once, says Miller. "If you feel, for example, that your spouse begins to hear you, then at least something is moving. Talk for 20 minutes and then take a break."

Ultimately, such practices work. As Willard found words for her anger, her depression lifted, her health problems abated, her self-esteem rose, and her marriage righted itself. She still has plenty of anger, but she reacts differently. Recently, she left work depressed about the disrespect she felt from one of her young male employees. But that evening she thought about how to handle the situation, wrote down the points she wanted to make, and then scheduled an early-morning meeting with him. "We still need to work on things, but it was the beginning of his understanding that I'm the boss. And I'm happy about that. Here I am in my late 40s, and I've finally grown up."

Anger Can Lead to Rages, Outbursts, Depression, and Physical Ailments

Liza Finlay

Liza Finlay holds a bachelor of arts degree from the University of Toronto and a journalism degree from Ryerson University. She has won awards of merit for her health and service writing and has contributed to Flare, Fashion, Chatelaine, The Globe & Mail *and* Hello! *magazines as well as online publications such as* Microsofthome.com *and* ellecanada.com.

Naomi Campbell versus her assistant; Britney Spears armed with an umbrella. From cellphone projectiles to spectacular battles with the paparazzi, it appears rage is all the rage these days.

And while I don't navigate herds of photographers or hired help, I can relate. I had my own mini-meltdown recently, when I witnessed a taxi narrowly missing a young girl at a crosswalk. I was so furious that I put pedal to metal and chased the cab down the street. Blocks later, I pulled up alongside the cabbie and screamed at him. He gave me a blank stare. Blink. Blink. He had no clue that he'd almost killed a child. And he thought I was demented. Possessed even. And I was possessed—anger had overcome me and I'd lost all ability to think rationally. I had been defeated by the dark beast.

Controlled by Anger

It seems I'm not alone in losing that battle, either. Most women feel controlled by their anger; they either explode like a volcano—spewing molten antagonism, leaving regret and resentiment in their wake—or implode, shoving anger so deep it eats away at their very core and wreaks havoc on their physical and emotional health.

In her 2006 study of 65 young women, Cheryl van Daalen-Smith, associate professor at the York University School of Nursing in Toronto, found the common perception of all study participants is that both voicing and not voicing anger has dire consequences.

"For all of the girls I spoke with, speaking up led to judgment, recrimination and shame," says van Daalen-Smith. "Their expression of anger made them appear unfeminine or bitchy. But not speaking up and denying their anger was equally bad, with the repressed feelings leading to depression and self-loathing."

To speak or not to speak—for Toronto psychotherapist Louise Giroux, there is no question. "Repressed anger eventually comes out as tears, rage or self-destruction," she says. "My practice is filled with women who have eating disorders but are really angry, or who suffer depression but are truly angry. Anger that is swallowed and ignored is the root of many mental-health evils."

Removing the Stigma

Van Daalen-Smith agrees: "We have to create a climate of safety in which it's OK for women to express their anger," she says, "but before we can do that, we have to make it safe for anger to have a voice. We have to remove the stigma associated with anger."

That stigma, says Giroux, has become entrenched through generations of blind acceptance. "Most 50+ women have been taught there is no redeeming value in anger, and we are rapidly passing that learning along to younger generations. We've been programmed to nurture, to fix, to care, to be kind and patient. If we're angry, we're failing somehow. If we're angry, we're condemned for feeling too much, for being too emotional. We're supposed to be civilized, and we've been socialized to think civilized people aren't angry."

In her book, *The Anger Workbook for Women*, Laura J. Petracek writes: "From an early age, women are taught that expressing anger is unacceptable to others and will lead to negative consequences such as being abandoned or having affection withheld. . . . Women's anger, therefore, is often misdirected in passive-aggressive ways such as sulking, backstabbing, malicious gossip, and writing someone off and never speaking to that person again."

Think about it: how often have you chosen to "vent" about one girlfriend to another, rather than confront? Who among us hasn't bitched to a co-worker about a supervisor because we don't know how to deal with that person directly? We know what we're doing is dishonest and soul-destroying, yet we do it anyway. Isn't there a better way?

Only anger that is unexpressed, that is shoved down, leads to rage, depression and physical ailments.

There is. If women have been afraid to confront their anger in the past, Giroux and Petracek both believe the era of the mad and glad woman is close at hand.

"Women are taking up more and more leadership roles, and as they do, they are redefining traditional stereotypes," says Giroux. "It used to be that an angry man was assertive and an angry woman was aggressive. That is slowly changing as the egalitarianism of the sexes really takes hold."

And the aim of therapists and activists, such as Giroux and van Daalen-Smith, is not to "deal with it," but, rather, to befriend it—hear it, acknowledge it and, importantly, act on it.

"The biggest learning curve for society is to make the distinction between anger and aggression," says van Daalen-Smith. "Anger is an emotion—a highly useful emotion that raises the red flag when something is wrong in our inner or outer realm; aggression is a behaviour." Denying that anger, she says, has far-reaching mental-health implications.

Petracek agrees. "Only anger that is unexpressed, that is shoved down, leads to rage, depression and physical ailments," she says. "When we talk about anger management, we're not encouraging the silencing of women's anger, nor are we promoting yelling and screaming. Owning your anger is all about listening to it, then learning appropriate means of expressing it."

Owning Anger

A vital first step is to legitimize anger: recognize the signs— the rush of adrenaline, the rapid breathing, the tight muscles, the flushed face—and recognize it as anger. Too often, says Petracek, women tell themselves they shouldn't feel angry. "But 'should' and 'feel' are two words that don't belong in the same sentence."

Giroux counsels her patients to take a deep breath, pause for a moment and reflect on the angry feeling: what set it off and, importantly, why? All of us have triggers, and identifying them is an important step toward harnessing anger effectively.

It seems I am triggered by injustice, particularly injustices brought upon unsuspecting children at crosswalks. I was pondering this hot-button issue a few days ago while driving down the same stretch of crosswalk-laced road. Once again, I watched a small child step off the curb and, once again, a driver (this time coming from the opposite direction) barrelled through obliviously, ignoring my honking horn and wildly waving arms.

Here's what I didn't do: I didn't peel after him, hurling insults. Nor did I tell myself I shouldn't be upset. I did, however, take action. I pulled over, hauled out my cellphone and placed a call to the local police, entreating them to post a crossing guard on that troublesome corner. And you know what? I feel better.

Sudden Anger Is Dangerous

Ronald T. Potter-Efron and Patricia S. Potter-Efron

Ronald T. Potter-Efron is a psychotherapist in private practice in Eau Claire, Wisconsin, who specializes in anger management. He is author of Angry All the Time. *Patricia S. Potter-Efron is a clinical psychotherapist at First Things First Counseling Center in Eau Claire.*

Explosive anger styles are very different from masked ones. Exploders know they are mad and they tell others about it. They easily become enraged. Exploders shout and yell, swear, throw things, break objects, threaten, shove, pinch, bite, and hit. . . .

Explosive anger styles have value. For instance, sudden anger has immediate survival value. Scientists point out that people's brains begin responding to danger signals within less than one second after danger is perceived. That allows almost instantaneous physical reactions, an excellent idea if, for example, the drunk at the next barstool is coming at you with a broken beer bottle. That's a great time for your aggressive instincts to kick in so you can protect yourself. Getting angry, on some occasions, then, may even save your life. At least exploders let the world know their feelings. But explosions are dangerous. People get hurt. Relationships get wrecked. Jobs are lost. . . .

I Just Lost Control—Again

Theresa's got a problem. She blows up like a firecracker, but not just on the Fourth of July. She blows up any time of the day or night, almost every day.

Here's what she says: "I'm in trouble. I lose my head just about every time I get frustrated. One minute I'm talking nor-

Ronald T. Potter-Efron, MSW, Ph.D. and Patricia S. Potter-Efron, MS, *Letting Go of Anger: The Eleven Most Common Anger Styles and What to Do About Them.* Oakland, CA: New Harbinger, 2006.

mally. Everything's okay, I feel fine. The next I'm screaming my head off at Joe or the kids. It's better at work, but last week I told my boss she was the sorriest excuse for a supervisor I've ever seen. She sent me home for the day."

When Theresa gets angry she feels out of control, as if she's being swept out to sea by a powerful undertow. "My God," she thinks, "what am I doing! Why do I say such terrible things: Am I losing my mind?" But she can't stop. Unplanned, unexpected, the anger seems to take over. And then it's gone. Poof! The anger disappears.

"Whew," Theresa says to herself, "I'm glad that's over." Sometimes she feels better, relieved. She's gotten rid of her frustrations, tensions, anxieties. More often, though, she looks around and sees the hurt looks on people's faces. Then she feels awful.

But here's what amazes Theresa. Some of those people she yelled at are still upset. They actually want to talk about what happened. Why? Theresa's not angry anymore. It's over. What's the big deal? Her anger's gone. What good would it do to talk! . . .

I Didn't Know the Gun Was Loaded

You're walking down the street, minding your own business. Boom! A bolt of anger smacks you right on the head. It makes you go crazy. You rant and rave. You can't help it. It hits so hard you explode. That's what people with sudden anger say it feels like.

Frankly, when we began treating angry people this sounded phony to us. How could anyone not see their anger coming? After all, there are plenty of warning signs that you're getting angry: physical changes, such as breathing fast and rising voice tone; emotional cues, such as feeling panicky or getting a headache; angry thoughts, like "I don't have to take this stuff anymore." All of these changes tell people they're getting mad. It was hard to believe anyone could ignore them. It sure sounded like a desperate attempt to avoid taking responsibility. "Don't blame me. I can't help it. I just get angry so fast I can't stop."

Later, though, we changed our minds. There are simply too many Theresas in this world, too many people who swear their anger catches them by surprise over and over again. We had to believe them.

Anger and the Brain

A tremendous amount of research on the human brain has been conducted over the last decade, it is evident from this research that some people's brains are simply not as good as others at controlling anger and aggression. For instance, some people have relatively weak activity in a place near the front of the brain (the prefrontal cortex) that helps us to control our impulses. Others have overactive parts of the emotional center of the brain (the limbic system) so that their emotions are felt extremely quickly and intensely. There are several other problems in the brain that could make someone more prone to sudden anger attacks. Medications can help people who have some of these difficulties.

People with sudden anger don't see any warning signs because they don't look for them.

You might need to consult a physician to consider an appropriate medication trial if you have been trying for a long time to quit getting so strongly angry but have not been able to control your temper. However, for the remainder of this [viewpoint] we will assume that you can learn to slow down your angry reactions with commitment and education. . . .

Nobody Gets Mad by Accident

Anger never just happens. It doesn't come out of nowhere. There are always warning signs, but you have to look for them. And that's the problem.

People with sudden anger don't see any warning signs because they don't look for them.

We've often watched the anger build up in people with sudden anger. They're really no different than anyone else. They make fists. They pace the floor. They worry and fret and mutter to themselves. Their eyebrows furrow. Their eyes narrow and glare. But there is a difference. Unlike others, they don't notice these signs. They don't realize their inner tension is rising.

Those with sudden anger don't know the gun is loaded. They don't realize the gun has a hair trigger. Worst of all, they don't even know they're carrying a gun. . . .

Frustration and Violent Impulses

People with the sudden anger style have adult impulse controls, but sometimes they seem to forget about them. Moments of frustration bring out the little kid in them. Ernie, [a] bus driver, is a good example. He throws his tools around whenever he can't quickly fix his car. Tim, [a] golfer, is a nice guy except when he's on the course. Miss a putt and he breaks his club in two.

"I can't stand frustration. I want everything to be all right, now!" That's how people with sudden anger get. They can't handle frustration. If they have to wait too long, or if they don't get what they want, they blow. Not all the time, though. If they tried that they'd be behind bars for a long while. Those with a sudden anger style don't lose control every time they get frustrated. It's more like playing dice. Once in a while they crap out. And when they do, watch out! . . .

Remember that people with sudden anger have been ignoring the signs that their anger is building up. They are frustrated, yes, but not only about the nail that won't go in straight or their spouse getting home late. They're also mad about the dog who barked this morning, and the cold soup at lunch, and the boss who wants three things done at the same time, and the slow crawl home on overcrowded streets. Too much stress. Too many headaches. And then they explode. No wonder their anger seems way out of line. They're taking out their whole day's frustrations in a one- or two-minute blast.

Impatience

People with sudden anger are generally impatient. They don't handle frustration very well. They're quick to blow up at themselves and others. Here's an example.

Beth's a single mother with three kids. She works long and hard hours at a poorly paid job. She hears demands all day from customers. Sometimes she'd like to shout at them, but she keeps on smiling. The one thing she wants is to come home to a clean house. But tonight she walks in on a pillow fight in the living room. What a mess.

"Alexander, pick that chair up *now*," Beth yells. "Rachel, take those pillows to your room."

"Aw, Ma, we're just having fun," they say. "Quit being such a grump." Then Rachel throws a pillow at her head.

"That's it. I said now and I mean now. You're both grounded for the night. You stupid kids. You know I work hard. All I want is a little peace and quiet. Why, you never think of me. You're just selfish little brats."

Beth raves on for the next five minutes. Then she throws herself on her bed and cries. And then it's over, except that Alexander and Rachel avoid her the rest of the night.

Impatience. Frustration. Violent impulses. Ignoring signs that anger is building. These are the Four Horsemen of sudden anger.

Beth is impatient, like most people with sudden anger. She wants things *now*. No dawdling allowed. She feels personally insulted when people are slow doing what she expects.

To be fair, Beth's pretty impatient with herself, too. She doesn't like things that take a long time to do. That's one reason she dropped out of school. And she throws down her sewing in utter frustration when she makes a mistake. She's often fidgety, nervous, and restless. She also does things without thinking, on impulse. Once she quit her job, just like that, because of something her boss said. She called up the next day and got her job back, but she got a warning to watch her temper.

Impatience. Frustration. Violent impulses. Ignoring signs that anger is building. These are the Four Horsemen of sudden anger.

Easy Come, Easy Go? Don't Bet on it

Ventilating. Letting off steam. It's one of the oldest ideas we have about anger. It's supposed to be healthy to let your anger out. You'll get sick if you hold it in. Just let your anger out, whenever you need to.

Ventilating is strictly an emotional event. Exploders are not solving problems with their anger. They don't first explode and then settle down to discuss their problems. They just want to release the tension that's been building up in their brains and bodies.

That's why sudden anger goes away so fast. It gets rid of a bad feeling. Ventilating sounds good. Why not let off a little steam now and then? But it can be a big mistake. Ventilating creates three major problems.

The first problem is that exploders often feel worse, not better. True, they're not angry anymore. But they feel guilty, stupid, out of control, childlike, irresponsible. Having a tantrum isn't exactly adult behavior. . . .

The second problem with ventilating is even worse. People with sudden anger use their rages for only one reason: to let off steam. They don't value anger as a messenger telling them that something is wrong and needs work. Getting angry is their solution to problems. But anger's not meant to solve problems. Anger is a great signal but a lousy solution. Exploders create many more problems than they solve by blowing up.

There's one more big problem with sudden anger. Every time you ventilate your anger you're just teaching yourself to be more angry. Carol Tavris, author of *Anger: The Misunderstood Emotion*, says that ventilating anger "rehearses" it. The more you practice sudden explosions, the more times you will explode. It's not true that ventilating anger makes you less angry. It helps you release your anger for a few minutes. But every time you explode you're training yourself to be more explosive. The madder you are, the madder you get.

People with a sudden anger style explode to feel better. But they usually end up feeling worse, making more problems, training themselves to get angry all the time.

Anger Can Lead to Constructive Solutions

Tori DeAngelis

Tori DeAngelis is a writer who has contributed to Psychology Today, Common Boundary, APA Monitor, *and other publications. She lives in Syracuse, New York.*

If you believe the Bible, the great philosophers and Chinese fortune cookies, anger rarely pays.

Yet the red-hot emotion has a positive side, say psychologists who study anger. In studies and in clinical work, they find anger can help clarify relationship problems, clinch business deals, fuel political agendas and give people a sense of control during uncertain times. More globally, they note, it can spur an entire culture to change for the better, as witnessed by the civil rights movement of the 1960s and the earlier women's suffrage movement.

"Imagine what the women's suffrage movement would have been like if women had said, 'Guys, it's really so unfair, we're nice people and we're human beings too. Won't you listen to us and give us the vote?" says social psychologist Carol Tavris, PhD, author of *Anger: The Misunderstood Emotion.* "To paraphrase Malcolm X, there's a time and a place for anger, where nothing else will do."

While there is no one definition of constructive anger—experts say it varies according to situation and context—psychologists are examining how its use can aid intimate relationships, work interactions and political expressions, including the public's response to the terrorist attacks of Sept. 11, 2001.

The concept of constructive anger is also gaining empirical support from a recently validated measure developed by Mount Sinai Medical Center psychologist Karina Davidson, PhD, and colleagues. Described in the January 2000 issue of *Health Psychology*, the instrument explores factors like people's propensity to calmly discuss their angry feelings and to work toward solutions. Indeed, use of the scale with male heart patients high in hostility suggests that constructive anger may have health benefits as well.

When you look at everyday episodes of anger as opposed to more dramatic ones, the results are usually positive.

Everyday Anger

Anger gets a bad rap partly because it is often erroneously associated with violence, experts note. "In fact, anger seems to be followed by aggression only about 10 percent of the time, and lots of aggression occurs without any anger," notes Howard Kassinove, PhD, co-author with R. Chip Tafrate, PhD, of *Anger Management: The Complete Treatment Guidebook for Practice*.

But a number of studies show that in the places where anger is usually played out—especially on the domestic front—it is often beneficial. "When you look at everyday episodes of anger as opposed to more dramatic ones, the results are usually positive," says James Averill, PhD, a University of Massachusetts, Amherst, psychologist whose studies of everyday anger in the 1980s found that angry episodes helped strengthen relationships about half the time, according to a community sample.

Echoing those findings, a 2002 study in the *Journal of Clinical Psychology* by Tafrate, Kassinove and Louis Dundin, found that 40 percent of a community sample of 93 people reported positive long-term effects of angry episodes, compared with 36 percent that reported neutral and 25 percent that reported negative long-term outcomes. Similarly, a 1997 study by Kassinove and colleagues in the *Journal of Social Behavior and Personality* found that 55 percent of a comparative community sample of Russians and Americans said an angry episode produced a positive outcome. Almost a third of them noted the episode helped them see their own faults.

"People who are targets of anger in these studies will say things like, 'I really understand the other person much better now—I guess I wasn't listening before,'" comments Kassinove. "While assertive expression is always preferable to angry expression, anger may serve an important alerting function that leads to deeper understanding of the other person and the problem."

Positive Feedback Loop

Several factors can make the difference between constructive and destructive anger, say psychologists who study and treat everyday anger. For one, constructive anger expression usually involves both people, not just the angry party. In the best-case scenario, the angry person expresses his or her anger to the target, and the target hears the person and reacts appropriately.

"If the anger is justified and the response is appropriate, usually the misunderstanding is corrected," notes Averill. Relatedly, anger can be constructive when people frame it in terms of solving a mutual problem rather than as a chance to vent their feelings, says Tavris. "The question is not, 'Should I express anger or should I suppress it?' It is, 'What can we do to solve the problem?'"

Likewise, it is helpful to understand that anger is contextual and social, Tavris adds. When anger fails to fill a constructive framework, however, it can morph into undesirable expressions of the emotion, anger experts say. Anger externalized can turn into violence and aggression; anger internalized can cause depression, health problems and communication difficulties, they note.

Power Plays

Anger also plays a powerful and arguably positive role in the workplace and in politics, finds Larissa Tiedens, PhD, of Stanford University. These are arenas, she notes, where anger is often used for status, power, control and strategic purposes rather than for emotional expression.

In a paper in the January 2001 *Journal of Personality and Social Psychology*, Tiedens showed across four studies that people grant more status to politicians and to colleagues who express anger than to those who express sadness or guilt.

And a study in [the March 2003] *Psychological Science* by social psychologist Jennifer Lerner, PhD, Roxana Gonzalez, Deborah Small and Baruch Fischoff, PhD, of Carnegie Mellon University, finds that anger served an empowering function following the events of Sept. 11, 2001. The first part of the study, conducted nine days after the attacks, gathered baseline data on a representative sample of 1,786 people concerning their feelings about the attacks and their levels of anxiety, stress and desire for vengeance.

The second part, conducted two months later, randomized 973 people from the original sample into a condition that primed fear, anger or sadness (the study reports only on the fear and anger conditions). People in the anger condition, for instance, elaborated on their feelings of anger following the attacks and viewed photos and listened to audio clips designed to provoke anger. For example, they watched Arabs celebrating the attacks. They then assessed the threat of terrorist attacks in the United States.

Participants primed for anger gave more optimistic—and, as it turns out, realistic—risk assessments on 25 possible terrorist-related risks than those primed for fear. For example, participants primed for anger estimated a 19 percent personal chance of being hurt in a terrorist attack within the next year, compared with 23 percent of those primed for fear. Because virtually no Americans were hurt by terrorist attacks in the 12 months following Sept. 11, the angry participants' estimates were more accurate, explains Lerner.

Anger is probably beneficial in this context because it increases people's sense of control, comments Lerner, who also has looked at this aspect of the phenomenon. In a study reported in the July 2001 *Journal of Personality and Social Psychology*, she and Dacher Keltner, PhD, of the University of California, Berkeley, found that angry people had a stronger sense of control and certainty than fearful people. That's not to say these tendencies are always justified or helpful, she adds: Angry people also are less likely than others to think they'll have a heart attack or get a divorce, when they're actually more likely to experience these negative events.

Lerner believes such studies have implications for the current "war on terrorism." They suggest that President [George W.] Bush's angry, tough-guy stance may affect public reaction by reducing uncertainty and increasing a sense of control, she says.

However, if the enemy continues to prove elusive, the tactic may prove maladaptive, Lerner speculates. "At the same time anger effectively provides a sense of certainty and prepares people for action," she says. "It also simplifies their judgment processes and leaves them prone to bias."

Anger Can Be an Alert That Something Is Wrong

Thoden K. Janes

Thoden K. Janes is a staff writer for The Record, *a daily news-paper serving Bergen County, New Jersey.*

The Hulk is all the rage again because of, well, all the rage.

Bruce Banner's alter ego, in fact, long has been one of the more popular Marvel Comics characters precisely because he is more primal and less complex than most of his superhero peers.

He's "just a big guy who goes around and throws [stuff], and punches people," said Jordan Raphael, co-author of the forthcoming book, *Stan Lee and the Rise and Fall of the American Comic Book.*

"[The Hulk's rampages are] kind of that great outlet that I think most people somewhere deep inside themselves wish that they had," Raphael continued.

But this is not Mr. Deeds, Billy Madison, or any of the other rage-filled (and completely unrepentant) caricatures featured in Adam Sandler's broad comedies.

[Anger is] an alert system to tell you that something is wrong and you must deal with what is wrong.

This is a "character who's constantly struggling to keep it under control, and when he lets loose, suddenly this dark, kind of monstrous incarnation comes out, and he has to deal with the repercussions of that," Raphael said. "I mean, yeah—I can think of no better metaphor for someone having to confront your own dark side."

We all have one, of course—everyone gets angry. Doesn't matter if you're the Pope or [*American Idol* winner] Kelly Clarkson, a janitor or a heart surgeon. On a regular basis, someone is going to infuriate you.

Society and Anger

And anger is more prevalent than ever. Corporate downsizing has made for angrier workplaces. Crowding on the interstates has made for angrier drivers. Television's promotion of win-lose situations (see any reality show) has flooded the airwaves with anger, rage, and frustration.

Yet it's completely normal to feel angry.

"Most people think that anger is a bad thing, whereas it's not," said Gilda Carle (aka Dr. Gilda), who conducts anger management programs for companies such as Citibank and IBM. "It's an alert system to tell you that something is wrong and you must deal with what is wrong."

The problem is, most of us are more prone to Hulking out than chilling out. We think, If I don't scream and yell, how am I going to get my point across? It's like you're damned if you do explode, because you're liable to alienate a friend or colleague; and damned if you don't, because if there's no venting, there's no release.

But experts say we shouldn't deal with our anger in such black-and-white terms.

Managing Anger

Instead of acting out or acting in, try acting through. For example: You're driving home from work, and someone tailgates you for a mile, then passes you on the right and cuts you off.

"You have to see the cutoff as being done to another car—don't personalize it," Carle said. "Then you claim what's really on your mind.... The issue [is] never the issue, it's always something else. And it's for you to figure out, 'Why am I really reacting this way?'"

Finally, ask yourself: "Are you ever gonna see this person again? Is this person vital to your life? If the answer is no, let it go," Carle said.

Experts say that we just need to identify what it is that is on our minds, what it is that is upsetting us, and deal with that in a calm, effective manner. Sometimes, they say, that means taking a timeout until the rage subsides.

Adds Scott Geller of Virginia Tech's psychology department, who researches anger and road rage: "Think of the other person as a person with a family, with motives, with aspirations—rather than just a barrier, or an object, or a means to an end. That can change your whole perspective with regard to personal anger."

Taming Rage

Although anger-management experts agree that a person's own rage can be tamed, the consensus is that it must be tamed by the individual experiencing it—not by an outside force.

By ignoring the angry person's rampage, you're unfortunately not making them any less angry, but you're also not exacerbating the problem.

"You can't reflect their anger, 'cause when you reflect their anger, you've got a vicious cycle," Geller said. "You just have to walk away."

Reason being, an angry person won't take well to condescension. An angry person doesn't want to be manipulated or analyzed. An angry person doesn't want to be told to calm down.

"They get defensive," said Michael McIntyre, an industrial psychologist at the University of Tennessee's College of Business who specializes in aggression, anger, and aggression research. "'It's not my problem, it's your problem.' ... Somebody who is truly aggressive, they've got all sorts of systems in place to reinforce that, and they're paranoid, they've got short triggers, they're under attack at all times."

When people are directed to anger management training, for example, they're angrier because they were sent there than they were for the original thing that they were angry about.

What does that teach?

"You see, what we have to establish in this society is to understand the need for this kind of training," Carle said. "Not just, 'OK, you're gonna get this kind of training.' But why do you need it? What is the need for that? That's the thing. And until people can establish the need, then why even bother to go through the paces?

"All I wanna do is help people understand what's going on inside themselves so that they can better cope and not kill each other. That's a simple request, right?"

And if all else fails, there's always "Hulk."

"Watching someone just kind of spazz out and go nuts," Raphael said, "is kind of a nice release."

Anger Can Be a Motivator

Deborah L. Cox, Karin H. Bruckner, and Sally D. Stabb.
Deborah L. Cox is a licensed psychologist and assistant professor
of counseling and gender studies at Southwest Missouri State
University. Karin H. Bruckner is an independent psychotherapist
and researcher in the San Francisco Bay Area. Sally D. Stabb is
a licensed psychologist and an associate professor of counseling
psychology at Texas Woman's University.

Real women use anger to their advantage every day. Ordinary women and extraordinary women make their dreams come true by accessing the power and clarity of their hottest feelings of opposition and their long-standing resentments. . . . Women who are very successful at channeling their anger into passion and creativity and helping others do the same with theirs, these women develop *their own philosophy about their emotional life.*

Rather than assuming the rules and conventions of their mothers or their therapists, these leaders come to their *own* understandings of their anger. They explain themselves in their own words. Sometimes they see their indignation and annoyance as a signal they've been hurt and have experienced a loss. Sometimes they view their attempts to repair that hurt as moving toward the other person, an attempt to get inside that other person's psyche, to understand what has happened so that they can make some meaning out of a bad experience. Some women say they make friends with their anger and come to know it like the back of their hand. Regardless of the words they use to portray their anger life, these exemplary women show us that it's up to each of us to consciously, deliberately write our own emotion rules and meanings and to live by them. . . .

Who's Savvy Now?

Once you were a little girl and you learned to control your hostile actions. You learned not to hit or throw rocks at people who ticked you off. You learned to avoid name-calling and derogatory remarks. You learned what was legal and illegal, ethical and unethical, right and wrong. These remain important, but now that you're a grown woman, you are ready to mature past these early lessons with the realization that anger and aggression aren't the same thing. You are ready to embrace and use your anger for your own good and the good of other people too. Dana Jack, a psychologist and professor at Western Washington University, once said, "A woman's development begins with an act of disobedience." For women, *growth and disobedience often go hand in hand*. Sometimes, disobedience means allowing your angry voice to be heard.

Do you notice yourself feeling less and less unsettled about being pissed off? If so, you may be well on your way to wholeheartedly embracing your anger. You move past your dread of anger, past the idea that you might become engulfed by your anger, past feeling vulnerable because of your anger or humiliated by your anger. You realize that even if your anger was prohibited or penalized earlier in your life, you can be okay with it now. You have little need for anger myths in your life. *This is anger consciousness at its best*; you understand where your ideas and reactions about anger developed, you can identify your own anger patterns, you aren't trying to divert your anger in any way. You welcome your anger as the adaptive and natural response that it is and feel good about it!

In addition, you have a real working toolkit of skills at your disposal when you choose to express your anger. You know you have choices about when, where, how, and how much. Does this mean you get madder than the rest of us or stay madder longer than the rest of us? Probably not. But you have less need to pretend you're delighted when you're really irritated, more tolerance for the honesty of your natural response, and more tolerance for others' too. . . .

You Can't Just Walk in Here and . . . !

Maybe you're still experiencing some hints of hesitation in your anger action plan. Being a woman and claiming the authority of your anger may still feel risky or unnerving at times. That's understandable. You're bucking the system and there might be consequences; but to be blunt, you do yourself a huge disservice if you *assume* those consequences will all be negative (which is what we are told we should believe). You won't know until you try.

The amazing thing is that when we talk to women who have chosen to move forward with changes based on their anger, we run into very few stories of unhappy long-term outcomes. In the short run, you may have to go through the discomfort of confronting a friend, changing a lousy job, alienating an abusive family member, or convincing your partner to go to couple's therapy. But the truth is, you *can* just walk in and express your anger in almost any situation. You have the authority to do this. Why? Because you are as fundamentally entitled to your feelings as anyone else on the planet—all of your feelings, not just the pleasant ones. No one can negate your experience. You'll hear people say, "You shouldn't feel that way" or "Your perceptions of that situation are totally off base." Don't let these arguments convince you there's something wrong with the feelings you have. Anger is your personal advocate. Now that you have anger's wisdom for company, you can make choices about expressing your opposition, doing it wisely and honestly, and trusting yourself to say and do the right thing.

It is critical to break the rules, to walk into unfamiliar territory, and take some risks in order to make changes that are adaptive for you. That's because the traditional rules and parameters for women's anger have largely been oppressive and dysfunctional and have held women hostage in bad relationships, unfulfilling work lives, and self-doubt. . . .

Order Out of Chaos

Chaos is commotion, disorder, the disruption of calm. When a partner is unfaithful or leaves us, when a friend betrays a sacred trust, when we are abused by someone we love, or when we fail at something we desperately want to do . . . all of these things bring chaos into our lives because they disarrange the parts of experience we expect and plan. And anger is a big part of this kind of chaos. Perhaps the most painful aspect of the kind of agony we experience when we lose a lover or a dream is the tumultuous sense of casting about, looking for a way to make meaning of, or organize a situation that feels like the end of the world. Where do we begin?

We can begin by letting our anger lead us through the most significant losses and to the most pressing issues—the most valued priorities we have. Anger organizes our thoughts and prepares us for the next steps. The things we're most furious about give us the opportunity to look into the future. . . .

Anger . . . can lead us to effect change in ways that go beyond our own small circle of experience to touch the lives of many others.

Change the World

Learning to acknowledge and live with our anger as a positive part of ourselves is transformational in so many respects. As soon as we accept anger as healthy and helpful, our perspective changes dramatically. We move from asking "What's wrong with me?" when we find ourselves angry to asking simply "What's wrong?" The problem needing to be fixed suddenly does not exist *only* within. Certainly, it's always worthwhile to engage in a little self-examination. But it's also necessary for us to raise our heads and look around to the people and communities surrounding us to find what needs change and improvement. We come to believe that anger is not a fault of ours and to know that when we are angry it is no longer our fault. Instead anger becomes a sign, an open door, a path that can lead us to effect change in ways that go beyond our own small circle of experience to touch the lives of many others.

CHAPTER 3

Is Anger Management
Intervention Effective?

Chapter Preface

Domestic violence in America occurs quite frequently and often domestic violence offenders attend a domestic violence treatment program that includes anger management. According to the YWCA of Glendale, California,

> More than 3 women are murdered by their husbands or boyfriends in the United States every day. An estimated 5.3 million cases of domestic violence occur among U.S. women ages 18 and older each year, resulting in nearly two million injuries, and young women ages 16–24 are the most vulnerable to domestic violence, experiencing the highest per capita rates of non-fatal intimate partner violence.

These statistics demonstrate how prevalent domestic abuse is in our society and that the majority of victims are women being abused by their male partners.

Defense counsels, prosecutors, judges, and probation officers routinely assign offenders who commit domestic violence crimes to programs that combine anger management and domestic violence treatment. The goals of these programs are to rehabilitate the offenders and improve the safety of the victims. The effectiveness of programs combining anger management with domestic violence treatment is debated among victim advocates, anger management providers, and the legal system.

Those that support programs combining anger management and domestic violence treatment believe offenders have anger issues and that low self-esteem, overreactions to imagined wrongs and rejections, immaturity, lack of education, and substance abuse contribute to the anger experienced by offenders. Clifford Strike, an attorney who has represented people charged with domestic violence crimes has stated that "anger management classes are appropriate for some offenders and efforts to interfere with their availability is counterproductive. . . . Discouraging an entire category of counseling could stifle innovation without conclusive research into what works." Currently, there are thousands of programs combining anger management and domestic violence treatment. Proponents believe that through such programs offenders are taught effective communication, negotiation, and problem-solving skills in order to cease perpetrating physical, emotional, and sexual violence.

Critics of programs combining anger management and domestic violence argue domestic violence is not a result of anger but is a result of the offenders seeking power and control of their victims, and therefore such programs are ineffective. George Anderson, founder of Anderson & Anderson, the world's largest provider of anger management counseling, argues, "The issue regarding domestic violence is power and control. The offender is likely to beat or abuse the victim whether or not he or she is angry." Critics also believe combining anger management and domestic violence treatment can lead to even further domestic violence because offenders are taught to focus on what it is that makes them angry. This type of treatment, they argue, is believed to result in the offenders placing further blame on their victims. Denise Donnelly, a domestic violence researcher at Georgia State University, contends, "It can allow the guy to come up with another reason why it's her fault." In such cases the physical abuse may be reduced but the emotional abuse is increased. According to Greg Loughlin, Family Violence Intervention Program Certification Manager, "The federal Office of Violence Against Women now forbids using domestic violence grant money to place domestic violence offenders in anger management."

Those undergoing treatment that combines domestic violence treatment with anger management often have additional mental health issues such as drug abuse, alcoholism, and distress from early traumatic experiences. These types of individuals also tend to have higher levels of depression, anxiety, and impulse-control disorders. Selecting the most effective treatment can be complex and should not be undertaken lightly. Unfortunately, it is not easy to identify whether a domestic violence offender suffers from dysfunctional anger or whether he or she simply seeks power and control over the victim. The viewpoints in the following chapter further explore the effectiveness of anger management in modern day society.

Anger Management Intervention Is Effective in the Workplace

Linda Wasmer Andrews

Linda Wasmer Andrews is a writer in Albuquerque, New Mexico, who specializes in health and psychological issues.

Turnout was good at Aon Services in Chicago when the company brought in a psychologist to give workshops on anger management. But Chet Taranowski, the company's internal employee assistance program (EAP) coordinator, noticed something odd: "A lot of people who came had someone else in mind. They were there because someone in their lives had an anger problem, not because they felt they had a problem themselves."

That's one of the ironies of addressing anger in the workplace. Employees certainly aren't oblivious to the hothead sitting in the next cubicle or standing by them on the production line. "But people who have anger problems don't necessarily recognize it in themselves," Taranowski says. "They're often surprised and shocked when someone confronts them with it."

In the past, many companies conspired with employees to look the other way. After all, confronting an employee in denial is a thankless job, and it's likely to make an anger-prone person . . . well, angry. But in a security-conscious world, this nonsolution is a nonstarter, so more companies are looking for ways to help employees get their anger under control. A 2003 Society for Human Resource Management survey illustrates this trend: Of 270 HR [human resources] professionals responding, 16 percent reported that their companies offered anger management courses to employees, double the percentage in 1999.

If an employer ignores warning signs leading up to a violent incident, it could be held legally liable.

"The real impetus for this growth came after 9/11," says George Anderson, director of Anderson & Anderson, a Brentwood, Calif., firm that has taken a lead role in training anger management facilitators. Recent, highly publicized incidents of workplace violence also raised the field's profile. "Then came the movie 'Anger Management,' which popularized it," says Anderson, referring to a 2003 comedy for which he served as technical adviser. Today, more HR professionals are looking for practical ways to keep a lid on workplace anger.

It's a Mad, Mad, Mad, Mad Workplace

Anger is undoubtedly a factor in some of the 1.7 million violent victimizations—mostly assaults—that Americans experience while working each year. (This includes incidents involving customers, clients, students and other nonemployees.) Employers that don't address potential problems could pay a heavy price.

If an employer ignores warning signs leading up to a violent incident, it could be held legally liable. "But even if the company has done things right, the cost of defending itself averages $700,000," Anderson says. Clearly, it's in a company's best interest to deal with hostile employees before they become violent perpetrators.

Fortunately, the majority of angry employees aren't assailants in the making. "Most of the people I see are not violent," says anger management provider Ari Novick, president of the AJ Novick Group in Laguna Beach, Calif. "Instead, they're simply people who have a difficult time expressing anger in an appropriate way." For some, rage is less an explosion than a slow burn.

"Yet even lower levels of chronic anger and worker conflict can increase absenteeism and decrease productivity," says Bernie Golden, a clinical psychologist and founder of Anger Management Education in Chicago. "It creates a less cohesive workplace and damages morale. Anger also competes with focused attention, so it impairs judgment and increases reaction time." These effects, in turn, raise the risk of critical errors and accidents.

Plus, intense or long-lasting hostility has been linked to medical problems—such as high blood pressure, high cholesterol and heart attacks—that may drive up health insurance premiums.

Stop the Madness

For employees who are always simmering, anger management training may help them control their feelings and keep them from boiling over into destructive behavior.

Many employees are referred to training directly by HR, while others come via their company's EAP. Since anger per se is not a diagnosable mental disorder, health plans typically don't cover anger management treatment. Instead, the employer or EAP usually picks up the tab, although some companies require employees to pay for it themselves. The training is typically presented in either small group classes or one-on-one coaching sessions.

Not surprisingly, group training is the less expensive alternative. Since the field is so new, there are no statistics on average fees nationwide. As a benchmark, though, Anderson says his classes generally run about $500 per employee: $70 for the initial assessment, $30 for a client workbook, and $40 per hour for an average of 10 one-hour classes. Anderson also provides one-on-one coaching, but, at $250 per hour, he says, most companies reserve this option for executives.

Despite the expense, however, some providers argue that individual coaching may be more cost-effective in the long run. "It can be tailored specifically to what that person's issues and dynamics are," says W. Barry Nixon, SPHR, executive director of the National Institute for the Prevention of Workplace Violence in Lake Forest, Calif. "People aren't going to reveal themselves as much with other people around."

[Anger management programs are] there to help people unlearn negative ways of dealing with anger and learn more positive ones.

Whether the anger management program consists of group training or one-on-one coaching, most providers space out the sessions at weekly intervals. Some also offer accelerated classes that cram several hours of training into a single day. At times, there may be pressing reasons for choosing this route. For example, Anderson has one large corporate client that takes its employees off the clock until they complete their training. Obviously, it's important to get employees back to work as quickly as possible. "But if someone were to ask me if I recommend this approach, I would say no," Anderson says. "If the option is there, it's best to spread out the training over time, because one key to good results is practicing between classes."

Anger Management 101

At a typical anger management session, you won't see people analyzing how their parents' botched approach to toilet training warped their personality. The focus of an effective session is on teaching people life skills, not providing therapy. Unlike depression and anxiety, anger is not recognized as a disorder in the *Diagnostic and Statistical Manual of Mental Disorders*, the main reference manual of the mental health professions.

"We are there to help people unlearn negative ways of dealing with anger and learn more positive ones," says Nixon. "You don't teach a person not to get angry—it's a natural emotion. The goal is teaching people how to channel their anger and how to behave when they do get angry."

Most anger management training incorporates skills such as stress reduction, communication, conflict resolution and problem-solving. In theory, this sounds like a good mix, but hard data on outcomes are lacking. "The effectiveness of many anger management programs is simply not known," says Jerry Deffenbacher, a psychology professor at Colorado State University who has researched anger for more than two decades.

One possible drawback to group classes is that it may be difficult to reach all of the participants. For example, class participants may include both people who are psychologically ready to change and those who are still in denial.

"These are two very different types of people," Deffenbacher says. "They may be equally angry, but putting them together in a common class may not be the best way to go. Also, there's good literature in other areas of psychology to indicate that, if you aren't ready to change, the intervention probably won't take hold."

Keep in mind that anger management training is geared to folks with garden-variety anger issues. At times, though, angry or irritable behavior may be a symptom of a more pervasive psychological problem, such as addiction, post-traumatic stress disorder or depression. Any anger management program should include an initial assessment that sorts out people who are likely to benefit from anger education from those who really do need therapy or medical treatment.

Warning Signs

How do you know when an employee might be a good candidate for anger management training? Some warning signs are relatively straightforward, such as being chronically irritable, impatient, short-tempered, argumentative or sarcastic. "Fellow employees may report that there is frequent conflict, or increased tension or lack of cooperation," Golden says. "There might also be increased absenteeism or tardiness."

Angry employees are found on every rung of the corporate ladder, from minimum-wage workers to top-level executives.

Be alert, too, for signs of "cold contempt," says Anna Maravelas, president of TheraRising in Arden Hills, Minn., and author of *How to Reduce Workplace Conflict and Stress.* "At work, a lot of anger isn't expressed by yelling, because people don't want to get fired or disciplined for it." Instead, some employees may express their anger in less direct ways, such as backstabbing, rumormongering and turf wars.

Angry employees are found on every rung of the corporate ladder, from minimum-wage workers to top-level executives. But according to Golden, one thing many of these employees have in common is unrealistic expectations.

"Let's say their firm is downsized, and suddenly they're doing not only their own job, but also the tasks of others who have left," Golden says. "They maintain the expectation that they will be rewarded for the extra time and effort." While that might be a reasonable expectation, it is not necessarily a realistic one in the current economic climate.

When employees don't get the rewards they expect, they can wind up disillusioned, resentful and angry.

Practical Pointers

Suggesting that an employee go to anger management training is one thing. Getting the employee to actually show up is another.

In some cases, you may be able to mandate attendance as a condition of continued employment—for instance, if an employee has behaved in a way that would otherwise be proper grounds for discipline or termination.

But a caveat: If the employee's behavior might have been caused by a "mental impairment" as defined by the Americans with Disabilities Act (ADA), you'll need to take special care, warns Karen Karr, an employment attorney at the Steptoe & Johnson law firm in Phoenix.

"If an employee acts violently, the employer may suspend or terminate that employee, even if the behavior results from a disability. The ADA does not require an employer to accommodate an individual who poses a direct threat," says Karr. But a dilemma arises when an employee whose behavior might be caused by a mental impairment merely threatens violence. Says Karr, "In this case, the employer may discipline the employee only if there is objective evidence that would lead a reasonable person to conclude that the employee is a threat to the workplace. Otherwise, the employer must accommodate the disability."

One way to gather objective evidence is with a formal threat assessment. If the assessment indicates that a particular employee is at risk for becoming violent, the employee may be disciplined—or, alternatively, sent to anger management training. Says Nixon, "If, as a result of the threat assessment, it's determined that this employee needs to work on anger issues, that is something the company can require."

In most cases, though, you'll probably be strongly encouraging an employee to go to training rather than actually requiring it. Often, the response you get may come down to how you present the situation. "You wouldn't want to enter into a power struggle with an employee who already has anger issues," says Steven Uhrik, an HR consultant from Villa Park, Ill. Instead, ease into the conversation with a few positive comments. Then state the problem, and be ready to back up your points with documentation. "Base everything on performance or attendance," Uhrik says. Spell out the consequences for continued problems as well as the potential benefits of addressing them.

"Document everything, but be careful about what you put in the employee's permanent record," Uhrik adds. "Use non-judgmental, behavioral descriptions of the employee's actions, and be able to demonstrate their effect on the workplace." Instead of writing that "the employee was referred to anger management class," Uhrik recommends using the phrase "appropriate company resources were provided to the employee." That way, if the employee's file is ever seen by anyone, including the employee or an opposing attorney, it doesn't contain anything that might be construed as defamatory.

Finding Help

Finding someone qualified to help your employees can be trickier than it sounds.

The ideal is a professional with substantial training and experience in anger management. But since anger isn't recognized as a mental disorder, strategies for managing it aren't a big part of the education that most mental health professionals receive. Therefore, it's important to make sure that people advertising anger management services really have the requisite background.

Do the company hotheads—and the company—a favor, and clue them in to anger management.

Anderson & Anderson has a network of certified facilitators who use its model of anger management. Also, a small group of facilitators and providers banded together in 2004 to form the American Association of Anger Management Providers. Both organizations offer directories of providers on their web sites.

In addition, since many anger management providers take referrals from the courts, Golden suggests calling probation offices or social services agencies for recommendations. Look for a provider who not only has the necessary education and experience, but who also does an initial assessment and has a well-defined training approach.

Once you've found a qualified provider, don't hesitate to refer employees when they need it. "Sometimes, just the process of identifying anger as a problem is a helpful experience for employees, because they're clueless," says Taranowski. So, do the company hotheads—and the company—a favor, and clue them in to anger management.

Anger Management Helps Criminals to Not Reoffend

Sarah Freeman

Sarah Freeman writes for the Yorkshire Post, *a national British newspaper.*

These are tense times. Tantrums, fits of pique, hysterics, call it what you like, but evidence of tightly coiled springs who need only the gentlest of pushes to explode into full blown rages is everywhere.

It came as little surprise when [in January 2007] Naomi Campbell, the supermodel with a super temper, was ordered to attend anger management classes after pleading guilty to throwing a heavy, jewel-encrusted mobile phone that hit her maid on the head.

But while Campbell, who has become used to allegations of bad tempered violence over the years, said she was genuinely apologetic and vowed not to let the incident "define" her; she's not alone in letting her moods get the better of her.

[In February 2007], Omar Sharif was also placed on an anger management course after he pleaded "no contest" to a charge of hitting a parking attendant, a hearing which came just three years after the actor and bridge player was given a one-month suspended sentence for head-butting a police officer in a casino near Paris.

Society and Aggression

However, while diva-like behaviour has long been an accepted trait of many A-list celebrities, tempers have also been fraying in the most unlikely of quarters. . . .

It's a trend which comes as little surprise to William Forde, a former probation officer turned children's author, who first began using anger management techniques more than thirty years ago.

"Today's society is more aggressive than ever," says the 64-year-old, from Mirfield, near Dewsbury, who firmly believes there's a place for learning anger management in schools.

"The problem is that we have encouraged people to become more assertive, to say what they think and there is much more freedom now than there ever was, but what people haven't been taught is that with rights come responsibilities.

"There's a thin line between assertiveness and aggression, but unfortunately that line has been blurred and there are more and more people who find they can't control their temper when they can't get what they want."

Just 10 per cent of those who attended [an anger management] course reoffended within two years compared to a national average of 60 per cent.

Coming to Terms with Anger

The seeds of Forde's own interest in anger management were sown when he was recovering from a car crash and trying to come to terms with the news that he might never walk again.

"I was 11 years old and it was very frightening," he says. "It was a really frustrating time and while I was only young, I realised just how much fear, anger and love affected how people behaved.

"Three years later, I was back up and walking and didn't think anything more about it until I started working for the probation service in the early 1970s and dealing with people who couldn't stop being aggressive. They had been behaving that way for so long it had become an involuntary reaction. I started monitoring their behaviour and the triggers for their outbursts and those three words—fear, aggression and love—kept coming up.

"They might have directed their anger against themselves in the forms of suicidal thoughts or they might have built up barriers which meant they couldn't recognise their inner fears, but all of them showed an inability to show love, because they hadn't been taught how.

"When a person is prone to fits of anger, the aggression is more often than not hiding deep-rooted fears and before it's possible to move forward you have to find out what they are. The real key is self-esteem. So many people find it difficult to see themselves in a positive light, but if they can't, then they will derail."

Abandoning Traditional Techniques

Abandoning the traditional techniques used in prisoner rehabilitation, Forde began to train himself in the art of anger management. The results, he says, were impressive; His own 10-year study showed just 10 per cent of those who attended his course reoffended within two years compared to a national average of 60 per cent and when he retired he didn't want what he had learned to go to waste.

"I ended up doing a lot of work with schools and began to write stories which tackled issues like bullying and disability," says Forde. "One of the most popular was about a dragon called Douglas who was friendly and helpful until he accidentally burned down his neighbour's house and, exiled by the village, he begins a campaign of terror against his former friends.

"It was used by therapists dealing with children who had been abused and I was just glad to be able to help."

The book has just come back into print to coincide with a stage version of *Douglas the Dragon* which is available to download from the internet free of charge thanks to a National Lottery grant.

"If we are going to tackle the anger and agression in our society we need to catch children when they are young," says Forde. "In an ideal world we wouldn't need books like *Douglas the Dragon*, but sadly I think the need has never been greater."

Soldiers in Combat Zones Benefit from Anger Management

Valvincent A. Reyes and Thomas A. Hicklin

Valvincent A. Reyes is a lieutenant colonel and Thomas A. Hicklin is a colonel in the United States Army Reserve.

A U.S. Army Reserve Combat Stress Control [CSC] prevention team was dispatched to Afghanistan in support of Operation Enduring Freedom to provide preventative mental health care to a U.S. Army airborne division and Special Operations forces. The team's mission was to ensure mental health readiness of units in the area of operations. In Bagram, Afghanistan, the Combat Stress Control team identified anger as a very prevalent emotion in the combat zone. Anger management interventions with individual and group counseling were implemented to help soldiers cope with anger. Of 7,000 military personnel stationed there during the team's rotation, there was not one completed suicide or homicide. This article describes how the 113th Medical Company identified, treated, and controlled anger at Bagram Airbase, Afghanistan, between June 20, 2002, and December 20, 2002, with anger management interventions. This article does not address the psychophysiological features of anger.

The Combat Stress Control Team

United States Army Mental Health has played a crucial role in ensuring a mentally healthy and mission-effective combat force. The mission of the U.S. Army Mental Health/Combat Stress Control team in combat is to maintain presence with the soldier, maintain the health of the command, save lives,

Valvincent A. Reyes and Thomas A. Hicklin, "Anger in the Combat Zone," *Military Medicine*, June 2005, pp. 483–7. Copyright © Association of Military Surgeons of U.S. Reproduced by permission.

remove the disabled from the battlefield, provide quality care, and return soldiers to duty. Historically, CSC teams were very effective in several conflicts, including Operations Desert Shield and Desert Storm and Somalia. After the tragic events of September 11, 2001, the U.S. Army responded by sending combat troops to Afghanistan. This CSC prevention unit provided several interventions, including command consultations, preventative mental health training, and individual and group therapies. Soldiers were treated for depression, adjustment disorders with depressed mood, combat stress, anxiety, and occupational problems. Anger was the common emotion. The team originally consisted of five members, i.e., two psychiatrist team leaders, each serving a 90-day rotation, a social work officer, a senior mental health specialist, and a mental health specialist. A psychiatric nurse, another senior mental health specialist, and a second mental health specialist were later operationally attached from a combat support hospital (CSH), bringing the total number to eight behavioral health personnel. The 113th Medical Company was attached to an airborne medical command task force in northeast Afghanistan and conducted treatment services near the CSH. Angry, dangerous soldiers raised serious concerns for the safety of other soldiers, because of the accessibility of numerous weapons in the combat zone. With the CSC prevention team, the treatment of psychiatric casualties and angry outbursts was performed on basic principles of proximity, immediacy, expectancy, and simplicity. Treatment was provided close to the front lines, with the expectation of return to duty. . . .

What Is Anger?

Although definitions of anger vary, psychologist Charles Speilberger stated, "Anger is an emotional state that varies in intensity from mild irritation to intense fury and rage. Like other emotions, it is accompanied by both physiological and biological changes; when you get angry, your heart rate and blood pressure go up, as do your levels of energy hormones, adrenaline, and nonadrenaline." . . .

Research involving combat veterans has shown that anger and rage are prevalent emotions in post-traumatic stress disorder. Soldiers in a combat zone are subjected to multiple stressors, including threats from enemy combatants, environmental hardships, and lack of physical comforts, which contribute to feelings of anger, frustration, and rage. Anger is mediated by the fight-or-flight response, which motivates soldiers to complete their missions. When anger becomes uncontrolled, however, soldiers become a danger to themselves or others, reducing combat readiness and effectiveness and the morale of the unit. When anger was the cause of combat misbehaviors, soldiers were referred to the CSC unit for anger management therapy. . . .

Symptoms of Anger

Symptoms are subjective manifestations of anger and were self-reported by the soldiers during therapy sessions. The team identified symptoms using a classification system . . . wherein verbalizations and behaviors indicated anger and aggression. Indirect behavioral symptoms were self-reported by the soldiers as feelings of difficulty with one's temper or impulses, depression, guilt, crying, tiredness, withdrawal, irritability, fatigue, or being accident-prone in the combat zone. Direct verbal statements indicating anger were comments of hatred, contempt, disgust, criticism, suspicion, blame, revenge, and self-hatred.

Signs of Anger

Signs of anger were objective manifestations of anger that were observed by team members during clinical assessments or therapy sessions. Indirect behavioral signs included clenched fists, angry affect, tearfulness, hyperactivity, difficulty focusing, and pressured speech. Assault-type signs were threatening, aggressive, or violent behaviors observed and reported by witnesses during the precipitating event, such as when an airman threatened to harm another airman in his unit while brandishing an M-16.

Cognitive behavior therapy is effective in reducing anger and depression, and it seemed effective for dealing with soldiers.

Verbally aggressive comments were statements threatening to harm either self or others. An example is when a soldier threatened to lose his ability to control his temper if his command did not allow him compassionate leave to visit his sick wife. Hurtful-type comments were statements criticizing others, intended to damage the reputation of others, and were made by soldiers who felt powerless to deal with others. An example is when a soldier spread malicious gossip about a supervisor he believed he could not communicate with. Rebellious-type comments were statements the soldier made that showed he had become angry with or had lost confidence in his supervisor and he would no longer follow the commands of his leadership.

Philosophy of Anger Management

The team used a cognitive-behavioral approach in treatment. Research has found that cognitive behavior therapy is effective in reducing anger and depression, and it seemed effective for dealing with soldiers with time limitations imposed by combat mission requirements. The treatment team maintained the philosophy that soldiers take personal responsibility to control their anger responses and to commit to behavioral changes. Therefore, we emphasized in individual or group therapy that one could choose alternative behavioral responses by developing a repertoire of skills to modulate anger.

Consequently, the focus in therapy was to help each soldier understand how he thought, felt, and behaved when angry. We assisted the soldier in committing to behavioral changes by recognizing causes of anger and in substituting anger-inducing thoughts with anger-reducing thoughts.

Goals of Anger Management

The team maintained four key anger management goals, i.e., cognitive, affective, behavioral, and restoration. In the cognitive area, the soldier learns that personal interpretations of life events cause anger. He is taught anger identification (identifying thoughts and perceptions that produce anger) and cognitive restructuring (thinking more realistically and optimistically). The therapeutic goal is to change anger-producing thoughts into anger-reducing thoughts by increasing problem-solving skills, realistic thinking, perspective, reasoning abilities, positive attitude, and hope.

In the affective area, the soldier understands the relationship between anger feelings and physiological processes and learns anger modulation (the ability to control anger responses). The therapeutic goal is to feel less angry by learning progressive relaxation, meditation, focusing techniques, and deep breathing exercises.

In the behavioral area, the soldier learns alternative behaviors to cope with anger. The soldier is taught anger management application, coping with traumatic events by substituting maladaptive behaviors with an adaptive, self-empowering repertoire of coping skills. The therapeutic goal is to learn anger control through appropriate behavioral patterns. The soldier is taught pain management techniques, networking for support, time-outs, exercise, avoidance, "counting-to-ten," and behavioral rehearsal with positive imagery.

In resolution, the soldier is provided assistance in establishing a support system for returning to duty. A "get-well" plan is developed with leadership to keep the soldier productive while maintaining overall unit morale and effectiveness. The therapeutic goal is to learn assertive communication skills, negotiation, and limit setting.

Our goals of anger management therapy were similar to those in a 1996 study of an anger therapy program using cognitive-behavioral interventions with Vietnam veterans with post-traumatic stress disorder and intense anger. The study showed promising results with anger control therapy, using a "stress inoculation" method to reduce anger with three main components, i.e., cognitive modification, arousal reduction, and behavioral skills training. . . .

Suicide and Anger

Afghanistan was an austere combat environment. Factors such as the fast operational tempo, extreme weather, unknown length of deployment, and difficult terrain, combined with individual genetic composition, developmental history, psychiatric illness or substance abuse, a significant emotional event involving feelings of loss, separation, or changes in the soldier's self-esteem, caused depression and anger, triggering suicidal behaviors.

As previously mentioned, there were no suicides at Bagram during our tour. However, feelings of depression, anger, and loss were common in the majority of diagnosed treatment cases in Operation Enduring Freedom (June through December 2002). The 634 soldiers seen in individual therapy were diagnosed with the following: depression (25%), adjustment disorders with mixed emotional features (25%), anxiety disorders (10%), occupational problems (20%), combat stress (5%), bereavement (5%), and others (10%).

In comparison, there were 17 suicides for soldiers deployed in support of Operation Iraqi Freedom (between January and October 2003). The same report of behavioral health disorders showed diagnosed cases of adjustment disorders (39.43%), affective disorders (including bipolar disorder, depressive disorder, dysthymic disorder, major depressive disorder, and mood disorder) (25.09%), anxiety disorders (19.35%), and others (5.02%). . . .

Group Therapies

The goals of the anger and depression groups were to help soldiers change their behaviors by identifying anger triggers and discover alternative ways of controlling anger in a supportive setting. There were seven group modules. The goal of the first class was to develop a definition of anger, for the identification of anger and for learning alternative ways of controlling anger. The focus of the second group was to discuss the concept of anger triggers, which produce angry responses. The emphasis of the third group was the identification of early childhood experiences and unresolved interpersonal/family issues causing anger in the "here-and-now." The purpose was the acceptance of the past and the decision for the development of an alternative set of cognitive responses and behaviors. The focus of the fourth group was learning to identify how anger results in negative consequences. The purpose of the fifth group was to identify personal levels of intensity that maintained anger responses. Soldiers were asked to identify how their anger responses were influenced by their parents or reference group. The emphasis of the sixth group was developing alternative anger responses. Soldiers learned behavioral responses most suited for their abilities. The focus of the seventh group was to practice alternative behaviors with group members who provided support for behavioral changes. . . .

Principles for Working with Angry Soldiers

The team minimized the risk of aggression by removing the firearm from the soldier. When a potentially violent patient was being interviewed, precautions were taken to minimize physical risks to both the therapist and the soldier. Before the interview, weapons were removed and secured in a weapons rack. A plan of escape was devised for the therapist. Two clinicians conducted the interview, accompanied by an escort. A "buddy," i.e., another soldier of the same rank, was assigned to provide support and supervision to the client. "Buddies" were assigned escort duty to and from counseling sessions, served as medical attendants during inpatient stays in the CSH, and provided escort on behavioral health evacuations.

Anger management intervention . . . was effective in helping soldiers control their anger.

A "no-contact" order was given to a dangerous soldier who threatened harm to an intended victim. . . .

All witnesses to the misconduct behavior were interviewed. Interviews with collateral witnesses to the crisis provided clinicians with a more realistic perspective on the soldier's working relationships and coping styles, enabling a more effective treatment plan. . . .

Findings

Anger management intervention based on the cognitive-behavioral approach was effective in helping soldiers control their anger. There were high rates of return to duty, low rates of behavioral health evacuation, high rates of attendance in group therapies, no suicides, and no homicides. A unified model of therapy seemed best suited for a combat environment characterized by a fast operational tempo, harsh mission requirements, and an accessible but undermanned behavioral health team (8 total for 7,000 soldiers). The reporting, accessibility to treatment, and management of misconduct attributable to anger were highly attentive and responsive because of several factors, including the high visibility of the forward-deployed CSC team and an organized collaborative system for trauma response (including unit ministry teams).

Conventional Anger Management Is Not Effective

Cecilia Capuzzi Simon

Cecilia Capuzzi Simon is a writer specializing in science and health.

At the age of 3, Steven Stosny was rushed to a hospital emergency room with a roof shingle lodged in his skull. In a burst of angry rage, his father had thrown it at Stosny after the toddler poked a stick into wall plaster that was still damp. Along with a permanent hole in his head ("Do you want to feel it?" he asks), Stosny was left with a vivid experience of the deadly potential of uncontrolled anger. Today, the 55-year-old Stosny—a Ph.D. and clinical psychologist practicing in the Washington, D.C. area—has become a multimedia guru of anger. He has turned his intimate understanding of the emotion and its roots into an unconventional treatment method that's gaining both widespread popular attention and the notice of other psychologists. Most anger management programs are based on cognitive-behavioral therapy and the premise that our rational thoughts shape our emotional responses. If you can think before you explode and use relaxation techniques to calm your physiological response, the theory goes, you can control your anger and its potentially messy aftermath.

An Alternative to Anger Management

But research has shown that conventional anger management doesn't work very well. Domestic violence [DV] treatment is even less effective. These programs can help the highly motivated—but most people with problem anger don't think they have a problem and don't seek out treatment. Besides, merely controlling the impulse to lash out doesn't get to the root of long-term resentments. At the heart of problem anger believes Stosny, are severe feelings of shame and guilt as well as a lack of empathy for self and others—or at least an inability to recognize and express it. Rather than merely teaching tactics to control anger, Stosny asks his clients to look at their emotional core and make a truly revolutionary shift: trade bullying for compassion. Instead of confronting angry people with their failures, he provides a way for them to adhere to their own internal values and meet their own best standards. Once that person recognizes his or her own best qualities, it becomes easier to substitute kindness and compassion for violence and hostility. "If you show people a way to change," says Stosny, "they do."

Anatomy of Anger

Anger is not a popular subject of study. It's not fun to be around, and angry people are difficult to treat. Inevitably, studying anger also involves taking on the conundrum of domestic abuse, a sensitive subject dominated by what Raymond DiGiuseppe, a professor of psychology at St. John's University in New York City, calls a "politically correct view" focused on sexual inequality.

There is no consensus on anger's roots or definition, and academics debate whether persistent anger, which usually accompanies depression or anxiety, is an emotional disorder in its own right. Nor is there agreement on how to help people deal with anger. Many consider "anger management" an empty buzzword. "I hate the term," says DiGiuseppe. "It implies that we can keep anger under wraps. It doesn't imply therapy or treatment for a problem."

Anger in Society

As a culture, we're ambivalent about anger. On one hand, there is a hip righteousness associated with flipping the bird at a driver who cuts you off, or, if you are a professional athlete, barreling into the stands to pummel the fan who has thrown a paper cup at your head. At the same time, we wring our hands in fear that anger is corroding civil society. But a moderate amount of anger, expressed under the right circumstances, plays an important role in healthy psychology. It saves us from predators, literal and figurative. Anger can motivate us to take on unpleasant tasks, like confronting a bully; it can maneuver others into attending to our needs. Besides, feeling anger doesn't always mean acting on it. Only 10 percent of anger is followed by aggression, points out Howard Kassinove, a psychology professor at Hofstra University in Hempstead, New York. "For a lot of us it's 'anger in,'" he says. "It's usually not shown."

Nonetheless, anger's provocations can be overwhelming and pervasive. More typical than physical aggression is the co-worker seething with disappointment and resentment. Even everyday hassles like commuting or struggling with an automated phone system can cause anger that manifests as stress, hostility, depression or physical illness. Stosny's lesson is that once the root of anger is identified, a person can learn to be less responsive to these petty frustrations—and gain control over what seems to be an uncontrollable reaction.

Treating Anger

"Most people with real anger problems think that something outside of them controls what they think and feel," Stosny explains in an interview at A.M.E. Reid Temple in Prince George's County, Maryland, where he is preparing to teach a class. "They see themselves as just reacting to their environment. I want them to learn that there's something in them that regulates their emotions, regardless of what other people do."

This night is the third meeting of Stosny's 14-week workshop. . . .

Tonight's lesson: HEALS, Stosny's acronym for the five steps in a process that replaces feelings of anger with feelings of compassion. It will be learned through repetition—what Stosny calls "emotional conditioning"—to be practiced at least 12 times a day for the next 12 weeks.

Those who want to change their angry reactions have to be wiling to unlearn deeply ingrained behavior.

His method has been shaped by John Bowlby's attachment theories and the teachings of Silvan Tomkins, who believed that all emotion is expressed physiologically. In his book *Treating Attachment Abuse*, Stosny explains that "a natural and healthy function" of shame or guilt is to help us maintain our attachment to loved ones: parent, lover, child. If we are threatened with loss of that relationship, guilt and shame motivate us to reestablish the bond, often through angry behavior. The problem is that anger is a turnoff, pushing the attachment figure further away, and making us angrier still.

Anger Junkies

"I've worked with more than 4,500 court-ordered DV offenders and child abusers, and I never met one who didn't feel like a powerless victim," he says—"No matter how victimizing they are, they see themselves retaliating against an unfair relationship or an unfair world." In this way, we learn from early relationships to blame our unpleasant feelings on others. So as adults, when we feel shamed or disregarded in situations that have nothing to do with loved ones—say, in the hierarchical workplace or in rush-hour traffic—our reaction is to get angry, targeting the person who made us feel that way. At the same time, we get a neurochemical rush from anger that relieves anxiety and provides a physiological boost. The nasty cycle turns many into what Stosny calls "anger junkies."

Anger experts agree that breaking this cycle requires more than an intellectual understanding, which is why cognitive therapy alone doesn't work for many angry people. Those who want to change their angry reactions have to be willing to unlearn deeply ingrained behavior. As Howard Kassinove points out, most angry people have been practicing being angry for years. Breaking such patterns in a 14-week workshop is a formidable challenge.

The Compassion Cure

Stosny didn't plan to study anger. Until age 35, he was a playwright of middling success and taught creative writing at the University of Maryland. Then his father died. His mother had left his father when Stosny was only 11, and the death plunged Stosny into deep depression. He struggled with resentment and at times felt suicidal. Eventually, he emerged from his depression with a desire to write a self-help book. Graduate school in psychology was the next step.

If you can replace the aggressive impulse with a compassionate one . . . you can begin to undo entrenched, violent behavior.

Through a fluke, Stosny wound up taking over an ill colleague's grant to develop a domestic-violence program. He was shocked to find little in the domestic-violence literature on aggression. Instead, he found mostly an antimale sexist litany. One of the two main methods for treating domestic violence, the Duluth model, is built on the feminist idea that domestic abuse stems from men's desire to control women. In Stosny's experience, that explanation of spousal abuse didn't add up. His instincts were right: Research on the Duluth model and on cognitive-behavioral domestic violence programs, the two main forms of treatment for domestic violence, shows that they are mostly ineffective and can even increase emotional abuse.

He sought out his mother for a reality check. His father's behavior was not a show of power, his mother said. "He felt powerless all the time," she told him. His problem, she believed, was an inability to experience compassion. Stosny went back to the psychological literature, theorizing that tapping into clients' capacity for empathy could provide an antidote to anger and aggression. "If you can replace the aggressive impulse with a compassionate one," he says, "you can begin to undo entrenched, violent behavior."

Dressed up with a little pop-psychology packaging, that's the basic idea behind HEALS. If it all sounds a bit New Agey, former clients swear by the process, claiming these steps enabled them to identify personal hurts fueling their anger and to develop a quick and automatic response to defuse anger's triggers. Some carry cards around with the HEALS steps outlined to remind them of its potential, or to hand out to others who have problem anger.

Applying Stosny's Technique

Don Freeman sought out Stosny after pouring boiling water on his partner during a domestic squabble. Some of Stosny's advice sounds "trite," he says, but it worked for him. "Dr. Stosny tells you to stop being a victim and blaming others for your feelings," Freeman says. "The idea of putting yourself in someone else's shoes—that's pretty basic. But staying conscious of that stuff helped me."

Judy Curl, a Baltimore-area therapist who works with troubled teens, took Stosny's workshop to understand her own anger, but she uses what she learned with her clients. One 15-year-old boy was in her office constantly for drugs, violence and aggressive language. No one could get through to him, and she was out of ideas. "I had just been to Stosny's class, and I said, 'You come across as really big and tough and angry. But under that anger, I think you're really hurt. I think there's a lot of pain in your family.'" The boy started to cry.

"That was the beginning of getting through to him," she says. "It was the only approach that worked."

The Critics

Among those who have devoted academic careers to the study of anger, there is skepticism, surprise and some envy at the popular notice Stosny is getting—including the appearances on *Oprah* and an endorsement by Dr. Phil, who highlighted Stosny's forthcoming book, *Stop Walking on Eggshells*. They are baffled, as well, by the growth of his practice (1,000 trained workshop teachers under his CompassionPower brand in 35 states and 15 countries).

Some are simply offended by his commercial success. Others criticize his method as a quick fix. No one takes issue with his basic idea. "What he says is quite sensible—compassion is good," says Raymond Novaco, a professor of psychology at the University of California at Irvine who coined the term "anger management" and is renowned in the field. And some commend Stosny for trying to find a new fix for anger—especially since he works with a difficult population that is not psychologically minded, and one that few psychologists want to treat.

The main problem is the lack of evidence. His work has never been stringently analyzed by an outsider, and researchers would like to see structured experiments and peer-reviewed articles that could scientifically establish whether the treatment is effective. "I don't give a lot of credence to [Stosny's technique]," says Novaco. "I've never seen his research published."

Stosny says he would oblige—if he could get the funding to do an independent study. He says he has been criticized in the past for carrying out studies on his own, and had funding pulled after being picketed by feminists who objected to his treatment model.

But Does It Work?

In 1995 Stosny conducted one-year follow-up research on 285 abusers who had undergone court-mandated treatments, comparing his graduates with those treated with a protocol derived from the power-centered model. After a year, 86 percent of his clients had not engaged in any violent episodes of pushing, grabbing or shoving, compared with 41 percent in the agency programs. Maryland's Department of Motor Vehicles also sampled 312 Stosny clients, comparing their driving records against a random sample of Maryland drivers. Two-thirds of Stosny's clients had aggressive driving records before taking his workshop. A year after treatment, 7 percent of the same group had traffic violations—three times better than those in the standard driver-improvement classes.

Julia Babcock, a professor of psychology at the University of Houston, says the time is right for a serious evaluation of Stosny's model. Babcock, who conducted a comprehensive meta-analysis documenting the weaknesses of domestic violence treatment, thinks Stosny's emphasis on emotions, alliance building and empathy is promising. But, she cautions, the jury's still out. "He needs a well-designed experiment to answer that," she says.

Practicing Compassion

It is impossible to disarm every trigger for anger in today's world, Stosny tells his class. People must instead learn to recognize the early signs of their own angry response—including physical reactions like muscle tension and increased heart rate—and moderate their reaction. . . .

If Stosny's workshops do nothing else, they are meant to teach clients that they can regulate their own anger, and recognize the potential in healing the pain at its core. It's not only a way for angry people to regain their equilibrium—it's the way we all learn to connect. "We survived as a species because of compassion," he tells his class, "not because of aggression."

Anger Management Intervention Avoids Personal Responsibility

Mickey Skidmore

Mickey Skidmore is a social worker and the founder of Turning Points Counseling Center in North Carolina.

For some time now I have found myself increasingly aware of being unsettled and uneasy about this "catch-phrase" expression which has made its way into the vernacular of our culture. In fact, I'm pretty sure that I'm downright ticked-off about it.

A day does not go by without everyday people referring to it: "I've got 'anger management' issues." And I wonder what does that mean? . . . exactly? Are you irritable because of PMS [premenstrual syndrome]? Are you saying you have a temper? You had a tiff with your significant other? You're mad because you came out on the losing end of a business deal? You stubbed your toe on the corner of the end table and you started cussing like a sailor? Your team didn't win? Does anyone besides me ever wonder about this?

To me, this seems like another step in our evolving process to further erode any sense of self-responsibility. Think about it. Everybody gets angry from time to time for one reason or another. It is an unavoidable part of the human experience. I suppose this expression helps us to dissociate ourselves from being responsible for the increasingly inappropriate, destructive, unhealthy and violent ways that we express and release our angry feelings.

Perhaps this "catch-phrase" expression acknowledges that we are actually socializing ourselves to be an increasingly an-

Mickey Skidmore, "Anger Management," Turning Points Counseling Center Inc., July 2003. Reproduced by permission.

gry and hostile society. There are plenty of sociological observations and trends that would lend [themselves] to such a theory. The absence of fathers in the family system, the devaluation of boys in our culture, and the level of violence in movies, TV, video games are but a few that come to mind, which negatively impact our developmental socialization process and model for us how to express angry emotions. As a result, our society is becoming ruder, increasingly short-tempered, disrespectful, irresponsible, angry and violent.

Anger Management in the Courts

Another aspect of this that really ticks me off is the recent development of court systems attempting to address this issue. In their sentencing, Judges are requiring people to get Anger Management, or attend Anger Management programs at mental health clinics. And once again, I have to wonder . . . what does that mean? . . . exactly? The conclusions I reach are that Judges are woefully misinformed. They seem to have bought into the oversimplified notions of the medical model. They must think that therapists have a magic 'Anger Management' bullet like physicians have pills for nearly any ailment they encounter. Not that this isn't an opportunity for someone to develop some type of service and capitalize on this trend, but in all my experience in the mental health field, I am unaware of any specific 'Anger Management' protocol. What I see mental health practitioners do in these situations is teach them a layman's version of Cognitive-Behavioral Therapy techniques. The other variable in this scenario, is [that] the state is shutting down mental health clinics. They are simply no longer willing to pay for such a service—especially if you happen to be an adult. (This is, however, a topic unto itself).

Anger Management and Mental Health

Mental health patients too have found it all too easy to buy into the trappings of the oversimplified medical model. Everyone today thinks they suffer from a biological disorder of the brain. And if not that, any diagnostic label or diagnosis will do. "I have 'anger management' issues because I'm bipolar" . . . or alcoholic . . . depressed . . . anxious . . . or because I'm personality disordered—as if such a condition absolves them of any responsibility when they become angry and express their emotions inappropriately. It is easier to blame the disorder or condition rather than take responsibility for one's actions. And now we have this expression: "Anger Management" that makes it all that much easier. And so, they would rather request drugs to sedate and manage these emotions rather than learn alternative ways to express their anger.

Anger and Society

Let's think this through a little further. First, what does it say about our society that we are turning to therapists to teach adults coping skills and how to express anger appropriately rather than parents teaching their children these tools during their development—associated with the values they choose to instill? Secondly, when people reach adulthood, after years of antisocial modeling and influence, what do they realistically expect therapists to do?

The recent movie "Anger Management" is yet another reflection of how this "catch-phrase" has made its way into our cultural awareness. However, I believe the movie was a tongue [in] cheek portrayal which used the vehicle of comedy to expose some of the deeper and more relevant issues touched upon in this article. After all, laughter is one of the best medicines when dealing with anger.

The real problem that we avoid is the gradual disappearance of the value of self-responsibility.

I submit the underlying crisis is not about anger at all, but rather a fundamental lacking and dearth of responsibility. Children (boys especially) receive powerful messages about responsibility (or the lack of it) when their fathers are not in their lives. And it is a disservice to teach children that the reason they "showed their ass" was because of their 'conduct disorder.' Anger in and of itself is not a negative or bad thing. It is an emotional resource available to us like love, joy, mastery, confidence and others. What and how we choose to express this emotion determines whether it is good or bad. The issue is rooted in our decision-making and critical-thinking processes (another dimension of our socialization process which is eroding)—the choices we make in any given situation—not the anger itself.

While our society may be growing increasingly angry, 'anger management' is nothing more than a passing, superficial cultural fad. The real problem that we avoid is the gradual disappearance of the value of self-responsibility. And if that is not enough to make you angry. . . .

CHAPTER 4

Current
CONTROVERSIES

What Techniques and Methods Are Used to Manage Anger?

Chapter Preface

Various techniques and methods are used to manage anger. Cognitive Behavioral Therapy (CBT) is one of the most commonly used methods to treat destructive anger. American psychiatrist Aaron T. Beck of the University of Pennsylvania School of Medicine founded CBT in the early 1970s. According to the Beck Institute of Cognitive Therapy and Research, "Cognitive Therapy is a form of psychotherapy proven in numerous clinical trials to be effective for a wide variety of disorders. The therapist and client work together as a team to identify and solve problems. Therapists help clients to overcome their difficulties by changing their thinking, behavior, and emotional responses."

The basic principle of CBT is positive thinking. People undergoing CBT anger management therapy are taught to change the way they think. According to CBT theory, feelings come from thoughts. CBT teaches that negative thoughts prevent people from recognizing opportunities and solutions to problems. Beck based CBT on American psychiatrist Albert Ellis's rational-emotive behavior therapy. Ellis believed distorted thinking stemmed from the assumptions "I must do well," "you must treat me well," and "The world must be easy."

People today are seemingly angrier than ever and routinely experience rage. In recent years terms such as road rage, desk rage, and air rage have become household words. Rages are often set off by something trivial that has occurred. According to the American Psychological Association, "Logic defeats anger, because anger, even when it's justified can quickly become irrational." Psychologists also point out that anger is often provoked due to power struggles between individuals. Power struggles occur when we are driving, receiving customer service, dealing with coworkers, children, spouses, the list goes on and on. Through CBT people learn healthy problem-solving skills and how to handle anger-provoking events. CBT therapy suggests that in order to avoid irrational displays of anger it is important to recognize physical cues such as a racing heartbeat and sweaty palms as precursors to anger. When physical cues of anger appear, CBT providers suggest using relaxation techniques such as deep breathing exercises and relaxing imagery to gain a clear perspective of the situation that is making us angry. Once the physical symptoms of anger are recognized people are able to evaluate what it is that is making them angry. CBT providers also point out that immediate solutions to problems may not be available, especially for complex problems. Instead of seeking immediate solutions to a problem, the American Psychological Association suggests the following CBT techniques: seek solutions to handle and face the problem, avoid jumping to conclusions, add humor to gain perspective of what is making us angry, and remove ourselves physically from the situation if possible.

CBT is used not only to treat people undergoing anger management but also those being treated for depression, suicidal thoughts, eating disorders, addictions, etc. Those who successfully undergo CBT learn methods and techniques that can be used to manage their anger. Self-help books, group therapy, videos, and software packages make CBT a cost-effective approach to managing anger. The viewpoints in the following chapter further examine various methods and techniques currently used to manage anger.

General Semantics Teaches How to Avoid Anger

Martin H. Levinson

Martin H. Levinson holds a doctoral degree from New York University in Organizational and Administrative Studies, is on the board of directors and vice president of the New York Society and Institute of General Semantics, and is the book editor for ETC: A Review of General Semantics.

Anger in the classroom is usually destructive. Whether from student or teacher, anger undermines the learning environment. It may lead to disturbing threats of emotional or physical harm or to actual violence. It can interfere with relationships between students and teachers, e.g., it's difficult for a teacher to be nice to a youngster who says "take a hike" or perhaps something more insulting. Anger can directly affect student performance. There is a clear correlation between anxiety and academic achievement: the higher the anxiety, which can be caused by hostility in the environment, the lower the achievement.

Many programs focus on teaching children how to express anger in socially acceptable ways. While there may be some benefit in this, general semantics (GS) can help individuals avoid anger in the first place. General semantics ideas and formulations applied to everyday problems offer a more efficient approach and one that puts less strain on the body. Anger produces changes in pulse, stomach acid secretions, and blood pressure. Anger can also weaken the body's immune system and make it more difficult to fight off diseases.

The general semantics ideas and exercises described in this article are ones that I used when counseling middle-school

Martin H. Levinson, "Anger Management and Violence Prevention: A Holistic Solution," *ETC: A Review of General Semantics*, April 2006, pp. 187–99. Reproduced by permission.

students in the New York City public school system. Elementary and high school students can also benefit from these ideas and exercises if they are adapted to the students' level of development. One does not have to be a counselor to use a general semantics anger-management approach with students. Teachers at my school were able to get good results with the approach when "teachable moments" presented themselves.

The Frustration-Aggression Hypothesis

Some theories on anger maintain it is an emotion caused by frustration. This notion, which has been labeled the "frustration-aggression hypothesis," states that when people are frustrated, the aggression drive is stirred up. The only way to reduce this drive is for the individual to act aggressively in some way. For example, Joe constantly raises his hand in class to respond to the teacher's questions, but he is not called on. When Joe asks for an explanation, the teacher replies that she thinks Joe knows the answers to the questions and she wants other students, who may not know the answers, to respond. Joe becomes angry and shouts, "That's not fair! Why should I be penalized because I'm smart?"

According to the frustration-aggression hypothesis, Joe became angry because he was blocked from his goal—to be called on to answer questions. But there is another theory that would posit that the source for Joe's anger is *Joe*. Rational-Emotive Behavior Therapy (REBT) asserts that anger is not caused by frustration but rather by a *demand* that one not be frustrated.

Rational-Emotive Behavior Therapy

If the frustration-aggression hypothesis is correct, then all "bright" students who are ignored by the teacher will become angry. But empirically this is not so. One can find "smart" students who become mildly annoyed when a teacher does not recognize their raised hands. Such students tend to think like this: "I don't like not being asked to answer questions in class but I guess that's the penalty 'intelligent' people like me have to pay with this particular teacher. No big deal."

Events don't cause emotions. Beliefs about events cause emotional reactions.

REBT maintains, as did the [ancient Greek] philosopher Epictetus, that "people are not disturbed by things, but by the views they take of them." In other words, feelings are based on thoughts, if Joe thought the same way his mildly annoyed counterparts did in the above example, he would not have become angry.

REBT, a system heavily rooted in general semantics, was originated by psychologist Albert Ellis in 1955. It contends that events don't cause emotions. Beliefs about events cause emotional reactions.

Our beliefs can be rational or irrational. A belief that promotes survival and happiness is generally considered rational. The following are some distinctions between rational and irrational beliefs.

Rational beliefs

- Can be supported by evidence or proof

- Are not absolute demands or commands

- Are desires, hopes, wishes, and preferences

- Produce moderate emotions such as sadness, irritation, and concern

- Help you reach your goals

Irrational Beliefs

- Lead to inaccurate deductions

- Are often overgeneralizations

- Are demands, commands, "shoulds," and needs

- Lead to disturbed emotions such as depression, rage, and anxiety

- Hinder you from reaching your goals

REBT maintains that the primary irrational belief leading to anger is the demand that "Things *should* be the way I want them to be." Anger is created by some type of demand, and that demand typically is formulated with words such as *should, must, ought to, have to*, etc. To avoid becoming angry, avoid making demands.

Irrational Belief 1: Things Should Be Quick and Easy

Many social scientists have argued that increased TV watching, with its quick-changing images and sounds, and the proliferation of modern time-saving devices that make tasks easier to complete, has led to an expansion of low frustration tolerance (LFT) in society. This phenomenon is manifested by an irrational belief that "things should be quick and easy." When situations don't conform to this demand, people get angry. But the "reality" of life is that things are the way they are; demanding that things be easy will not make them easy; and many things in life are quite difficult.

To help students that I counseled become more tolerant of life's frustrations, I introduced them to Alfred Korzybski's *extensional theory of happiness*. This theory contends that to reach a level of contentment in life we should place realistic expectations on situations, work hard, and be prepared to *not* find exactly what we want. Another idea that helped students deal better with frustration was this: try to figure out what caused the frustration and see if that can be changed. The general semantics *delayed reaction* technique (investigate what is going on before acting) supported them in doing this. . . .

Irrational Belief 2: People Should Love and Approve of Me

Most of us want to be loved and approved of by others; for young people, because of their immaturity, these desires are particularly acute. To satisfy such wants they often make intense efforts to join cliques or curry favor with peers. If their exertions in these endeavors fail, anger (at the rejecting groups or individuals) or depression (self-anger) often results.

To help students to not react to rejection with anger or depression, I acquainted them with the idea of self-acceptance. (People who accept themselves, regardless of how others view them, are much more likely to experience minimum amounts of anxiety, anger, and depression.) I also discussed the rational belief that it makes sense to *prefer* things go our way, rather than *demand* they do.

Other people cannot control our emotions, unless we let them.

If we prefer that people love and approve of us, and they don't, we will probably be disappointed, sad, and annoyed. But if we demand love and approval, and it is not forthcoming, then intense feelings of depression and anger are likely to occur. Changing a *demand* (I must have it this way) to a *preference* (I would like to have it this way but if things don't work out I can still survive and be happy) can help us to stay calm and composed. That state of mind is typically more productive for moving forward in life than feeling miserable or irate that things didn't turn out the way we thought they should.

Irrational Belief 3: Other People Make Me Angry

Because feelings are based on thoughts, we have power over our emotions. The irrational belief that other people have the ability to make us angry gives control of our emotions over to them. In doing this we set ourselves up as targets for emotional button pushers.

To rid students of the irrational belief that "other people make me angry," I invited them to behave like scientists and perform the following experiment: "Take this checklist of types of responses. Survey thirty of your classmates and ask them how they feel when someone gives them a 'dirty look.' Match the responses they give you to the categories on your checklist and review the results." The checklist categories were (a) angry (b) indifferent (c) curious (d) some other response. Invariably, the variety of survey answers showed that people do not have to become angry when given a dirty look.

We are responsible for our own feelings. We are not robots, subject to the whims of evil robot masters at the "emotional controls."

The fact is we can *choose* to become angry if we are given a dirty look, or called a "bad name," or subjected to other sorts of "offenses." But the choice is ours. Other people cannot control our emotions, unless we let them.

Another exercise I did with the students was to give a youngster a piece of paper with the word "jerk" written on it. I then asked the student, "Did I make you into a jerk by giving you that paper?" (The student would answer "No.") "Can a mere word magically change you into something you are not?" (The student again would answer "No.") "Then how smart is it to let someone else rule your behavior through name-calling?"

After this exercise, we discussed the point that one does not have to impulsively react to words. We can select our reactions to situations depending on how we view them. We are responsible for our own feelings. We are not robots, subject to the whims of evil robot masters at the "emotional controls."

Irrational Belief 4: I Must Have Certainty in My Life

Because we live in a process world, where things are constantly changing, it is impossible to have events always turn out the way we want them to. Demanding that they should is a surefire way to become angry.

To help my "counselees" accept the rational belief that *uncertainty* is the norm in life I acquainted them with the Greek philosopher Heraclitus' idea that you cannot step twice into the same river. I also brought up T.S. Eliot's observation, from *The Cocktail Party*, that "what we know of other people is only the memory of the moments during which we knew them. And they have changed since then . . . At every moment we are meeting a stranger." And I spoke about a GS notion known as the *General Principle of Uncertainty*.

The General Principle of Uncertainty (GPU), a generalization of the more restricted uncertainty principle as formulated in physics, states that because our nervous systems and all events in life are unique, statements describing situations can only be made in terms of probability. For example, "There is an 85% likelihood that 'x' will happen." "I am *almost* sure that 'y' will occur." The GPU is a rational counterbalance to the idea of absolute certainty.

This counterbalance is based on the scientific view of chance. Because of the possibility of chance, the concept of absolute certainty does not exist in science. Events are relative. To stay on a fairly even keel, general semantics recommends learning to live with the "relatives."

Irrational Belief 5: I Must Do Well in Everything That I Try

The irrational demand to do well in everything one tries can result in anger if one does less than well in a particular activity. A more rational conception is that "doing" is more important than doing well. [Author] G.K. Chesterton went so far as to say, "If a thing is worth doing, it is worth doing badly."

People have many skills and abilities. Success does not make an individual worthy and failure does not make an individual worthless. It is far more rational to accept a person as intrinsically valuable and meritorious than to link a person's value with his or her achievements. People are far too complex to be given ratings, or to rate themselves, on all aspects of their lives. Who would decide which aspects are the most meaningful? Are verbal skills more important than mechanical skills?

Revenge is unproductive for attaining constructive relationships and peace of mind.

It is true that one can "objectively" measure failure in an activity, e.g., you score 40% on an English exam or you lose a tennis match. But when you define yourself as "a failure" you are engaging in what philosopher Bertrand Russell calls a "category error." The things you fail at are in one category and you, the doer of those things, are in a different category. We all have various levels of mastery in the projects we undertake. When we categorize our performances as "successes" or "failures" and then categorize ourselves, the doers, as "successes" or "failures" because of our performances, we have confused one category with another. We are not what we do. Consequently, it is sensible to rate only the things we do and not identify them with who we are, which is quite a different category. . . .

Irrational Belief 6: I Must Seek Revenge for Past Harms

The idea that revenge is sweet is fairly prevalent in our society. But typically revenge begets revenge and this can escalate—you hurt me, I hurt you, you get back at me for hurting you. I get back at you for hurting me, etc. Revenge is unproductive for attaining constructive relationships and peace of mind.

People who become angry and seek revenge frequently do so because they feel they have been embarrassed or humiliated (their anger is a cover-up for these feelings). Being assertive, letting others know how we feel, can often prevent such an emotional spiral. (Another benefit of being assertive is that standing up for oneself, in a socially acceptable manner, makes it less likely that one will be taken advantage of.)

I found that training students in assertiveness skills (e.g., expressing feelings directly, expressing what one would like, respecting the rights of others) helped them to resolve problems and avoid cravings for retribution. For example, Mary insulted Jane in the school cafeteria. Jane, who had taken assertiveness training, told Mary she felt hurt by the remark and that it was uncalled for. Mary apologized for her insensitive comment and the incident came to a happy conclusion.

Becoming More Aware of Oneself Can Help Manage Anger

Steve Cutting

Steve Cutting is a native of western Massachusetts who enjoys writing and is interested in men's issues.

Anger is all the rage today. We have "road rage," "air rage," "supermarket rage," even "public bathroom rage." It sounds kind of funny, but for many people, including myself, problems with controlling rage and impulsive anger are nothing to laugh about.

Unhealthy anger may be a problem for both sexes, but I'm going to focus on men's anger, and suggest that by taking a look at what may lie behind our destructive anger, men have the potential to stop or at least reduce undesirable behavior that causes problems in their lives. By summoning the courage to look at the shadowy aspects of ourselves, we can experience personal transformation; we can rebalance our lives and become clearer, calmer, more accepting individuals. We can become builders instead of destroyers.

Consequences of Anger

A recent flyer for a course in anger management offered by the Men's Resource Center for Change [MRC] in Amherst, Mass., open to both men and women, contains this advisory: "Destructive anger can wreak havoc in a man's life—resulting in ruined relationships, job loss, physical endangerment, health problems and trouble with the law."

How true that is. About four years ago [in 2002] I moved to western Massachusetts to be closer to relatives when after

Steve Cutting, "Finding the Way Through," *Voice Male*, Fall 2006. Reproduced by permission.

the birth of our child, my wife was diagnosed with a degenerative neuromuscular condition, severely limiting her physical movement. Aside from being a great personal burden to her, my wife's illness became an issue for us when the Department of Social Services [DSS] intervened out of concern that her condition might limited her ability to be an effective parent. DSS also raised concerns that I had not been emotionally supportive to my wife, that I had frequently lost my temper, and that I had behaved inappropriately, even abusively, at times during our marriage.

After a long and contentious struggle, a family court interceded and concluded that our child would be better served by an In-Family Open Adoption. Fortunately, my younger brother and his wife were only too willing to adopt our child. Presently our child is doing well in my brother's family, with two older, previously adopted siblings who seem to adore him. Because the adoption is in my family, I am fortunate to have contact and frequent visits with our child.

Not so fortunate was our marriage. After the adoption, my wife and I were unable to work out our differences and have since separated and divorced.

I chose to respond to these stresses with impulsive rage and anger—which has had painful consequences.

I have to say that I am truly sorry for the hurt I caused my ex-wife. She and I are at peace with our decision to separate and have accepted the decision to place our child for adoption as the most appropriate choice under difficult circumstances. On the other hand, the pain of losing custody of my child has given me the opportunity to reexamine choices I made in the past, both in my marriage and in other areas of life.

I made choices with respect to managing stress, frustration, and not getting what I want in certain circumstances that were inappropriate. At times I chose to respond to these stresses with impulsive rage and anger—which has had painful consequences and led to a period of loss and sadness in my life. Ironically, however, the experience of feeling sadness and grief over the consequences of my own behavior has been a necessary step toward understanding and changing it.

After losing the right to be my child's parent, I was already suffering from self-doubt and a fairly serious depression. After my wife moved out, even though I intuitively understood it to be the right thing, my depression deepened. As it turned out, her leaving, as painful as it was, became the beginning of a kind of catalyst for change where I gradually began to perceive things differently. Although it wasn't by choice, for the first time in a number of years I began to spend a great deal more time alone, providing an opportunity to reflect on the repercussions of choices I had made. This time became a kind of vehicle for change and helped shift my focus inward toward the source of my own personal turmoil and angst, rather than outward toward blaming external circumstances.

Through meditation we learn to quietly observe uncomfortable bodily sensations and unsettling thoughts by letting them pass through.

Buddhism and Anger Management

As a way of dealing with anger I began to pay more attention to Buddhism, which I had been aware of, but never seriously looked at. The first of the Four Noble Truths of Buddhism—Life is suffering—took on an ironic sort of attraction to me because it directly contradicted everything I had been conditioned to believe. The Buddhist principle of the impermanence of all things helped me understand my experience and provided some relief from the deep changes and personal losses I had endured.

Coincidentally, in one of my more desperate moments, at a relative's house I came across the book *When Things Fall Apart*, a brief encapsulation of Tibetan Buddhism by American Buddhist nun Pema Chödrön. One of Chödrön's key hypotheses is that often, only through life's most difficult and painful experiences, if we can courageously look at them, can the process of alchemy take place that brings about insight, which leads to the wisdom to change. The essential message of the book is that by "staying" with the unease often created by life's challenges—relationships, work, all areas of our experience—and not turning away, the fear becomes less threatening. As we sit with the unease, over time it becomes more familiar and thus less menacing to us. In Chödrön's words we become "Spiritual Warriors," gaining confidence and fearlessness as we move forward with anticipation and greater certainty into the uncharted waters of our future.

Recognizing Anger

At the same time, I began regularly attending the MRCs evening drop-in men's support groups, where the topics discussed aren't limited to anger, and where I continue to find enormous camaraderie and support. I also began taking the anger management course I mentioned earlier, and that helped me a great deal as well. Now, when I feel symptoms of anger coming on—increased muscle tension, shallow breathing, judgmental thoughts—I treat them as a warning signal. They become almost a road sign, directing me to turn my attention inward. This process helps unmask the negative sensations for what they truly are: misperception and fictions created by an overly analytical, ruminating mind. As Buddhism teaches, through meditation we learn to quietly observe uncomfortable bodily sensations and unsettling thoughts by letting them pass through, and not attaching to them. I have found that these "thought stopping" techniques, and meditation, help to better manage my anxiety and depression, as well as to curb my tendency to respond impulsively with knee jerk explosive anger when faced with inevitable frustration and disappointment.

If you suspect, as I do, that precipitous anger may be in part caused by fear—particularly for men whose early impressions of manhood are often based on unrealistic ideals of invincible comic book character types and John Wayne-style superheroes who display dazzling feats of machismo in the face of adversity—then it follows that for men, being able to look fearlessly at their weaknesses, uncertainties, and vulnerabilities may be a key to unlocking the prison of their hurtful anger.

I've found that truly feeling the suffering and regret that may go with accepting responsibility for the consequences of one's destructive anger is a necessary step if the anger is to be transformed. The methods mentioned above do not offer an easy fix and change does not necessarily come about quickly, but I believe if one can muster the courage to look at the shadowy side of one's own psyche, then the journey is worth it. Looking at these issues, painful as they are, has helped me in the struggle to control my anger and change my behavior. It's been a difficult process at times, but through it all I have learned that with consistent effort, real personal growth is possible.

Traditional Anger Management Courses Help Control Anger

Steve Farrar

Steve Farrar writes for The Times *of London.*

Steve Spicer was determined to focus on the needs of his customers. Even when negotiations were difficult, the 31-year-old customer-delivery manager at an American engineering group would remain outwardly calm. Nonetheless, Spicer admitted that he would sometimes get stressed and "take it out on the staff".

[In 2007], during his annual appraisal, his boss suggested he should go on an anger-management course. Spicer was taken aback. "It's quite an embarrassing area of personal development," he said. "I was also nervous that I would be joining a bunch of nutters [mentally ill people] but, in fact, it was brilliant."

Benefits of Anger Management

The two-day course, run by Reed Learning, gave Spicer an insight into how he might channel his emotions in more productive ways. "I got all these different techniques to stop me biting someone's head off, stop me from reacting to situations in the wrong way," he said.

"I can now step back, look at what I'm doing and not get stressed—I have become very methodical when trying to work out how to solve situations."

Spicer had a better appraisal [the next] year and there has been talk of him taking on greater responsibility.

As many professionals progress up the career ladder, they become more stressed. Some respond with anger, others anxiety—reactions that can stand in the way of ambition regardless of an individual's technical abilities.

Wendy Brooks, a director of the training firm Hemsley Fraser, said that the realities of management and leadership required people to be able to manage ever greater scale, complexity and uncertainty. This often threw up emotional challenges.

"When people are making career transitions, seeking promotions and moving into middle and senior management, underlying aspects of you are going to come to the fore," she said. "It will hold you back if you cannot grow in terms of leadership resilience."

But training and coaching can make a difference. At Hemsley Fraser, Brooks said the focus was not so much on tackling personal issues as on building on an individual's strengths in leadership resilience. One-on-one counselling and courses could reveal why individuals were becoming stressed and help them to take the emotion out of the situations that could trigger problems.

The upshot of this is that managers can become better at dealing with bigger problems and achieve results faster. This can improve their career prospects.

Anger Management Success

Nevertheless, discussing such issues remains taboo, with many of the professionals who spoke to *The Sunday Times* about their experiences requesting anonymity. Paul Smith (not his real name) is the operations director of a security firm that will turn over between [8 million and 10 million pounds Sterling in 2008]. Smith draws a salary of £100,000. He attended a two-day course organised by Hemsley Fraser to help him deal with stress.

"Before, I wouldn't take other people's feelings or the impact of my actions into account," he said. "I returned from the course really excited and regretful that I had not taken it years ago."

Smith's colleagues have noticed the difference, and the atmosphere at work has improved. His staff trust him more and seem better motivated. They even involve him in their jokes.

"When things get particularly stressful, they say I remain calm now," he said.

Another man who was prone to flying off the handle was John Roberts (not his real name), managing director of the British subsidiary of a European construction company. "I could take things very personally, get angry and then deal with problems in ways that were not appropriate and measured. Later, I would realise that I had upset and hurt people," said Roberts. "I didn't want to go into the office and the staff didn't want me to either. It was all getting too much and I knew it had to stop."

Roberts signed up for a three-day course run by the British Association of Anger Management. Despite his cynicism, he described the training as "inspirational". He learnt how and why he became angry as well as how to channel his feelings so that he did not hurt people. "The most important thing I learnt was not to take things so personally," he said.

Roberts then promoted several colleagues so they could take more responsibility, spreading the burden of much of the work-related stress. As his attitude changed, staff morale rose and people asked what had changed him—Roberts has told only a couple of his colleagues about the course.

"Without it, I would have probably damaged my career, possibly even quit," he said. "Now I'm really enthusiastic again."

Cary Cooper, professor of organisational psychology and health at Lancaster University, agreed that training could help but argued that usually learning how to channel anger more effectively offered only a short-term solution.

"It's important that any kind of anger-management programme should also explore why you have the anger and try to deal with that," he said.

Cooper said anger was usually a sign of workplace stress, which was often caused by too few people doing too much work, an imbalance between home and work and the impact of changing performance targets.

Cooper suggested that, rather than sending individuals for counselling, it might be more effective for an organization to carry out a stress audit to find out what was causing the anger.

Nutritional Therapy May Help Reduce Anger

Laura Potts

Laura Potts graduated in 2000 from Michigan State University with a degree in journalism and works for the Detroit Free Press.

Like a child reciting his favorite video game titles, Dylan DeGlopper meticulously lists the foods he can't have: anything with wheat or white flour; flavored popcorn and potato chips; anything enhanced with smoky seasoning. The no-nos go on and on.

But breads, cookies, beef jerky and more aren't off limits for weight-control reasons. For Dylan, the foods fuel his aggression, anger, irritability and instability. If the Kalamazoo, Mich., 12-year-old eats ordinary foods that contain wheat, MSG or other common ingredients, he said his "head feels tingly and lightheaded, and then it's like a big burst of feeling everything."

"I was ornery and cranky," he said recently, four months after starting a gluten-free diet. "I feel a lot better than I did when I was eating normal stuff. Now with this, I feel a lot more mellow."

As advances are made into understanding children's emotional and mental disorders, some experts are espousing nontraditional, holistic approaches to treatment, such as the nutritional therapy Dylan is trying.

Nutritional Therapy Progress

"It's easy to throw a medication at something but understanding what the real, underlying cause is takes a lot more legwork," said Constantine Bitsas, executive director of the Health

Research Institute Pfeiffer Treatment Center in Warrenville, Ill. The nonprofit research and treatment facility specializes in researching biochemical imbalances that affect mental health. It purports to have treated more than 16,000 patients with behavior dysfunctions, depression, schizophrenia, bipolar disorder, autism, learning disorders or anxiety by balancing body and brain chemistry.

Bitsas, who has a degree in psychology [from] Portland State University in Oregon and was a mental health therapist for eight years, said most people's bodies have no problem breaking down glutens. But for those like Dylan who can't, the proteins act like opiates, causing a lack of focus and an inability to pay attention, stay on task and think clearly. Glutens also can cause sugar levels to go up and down, leading to irritability and aggression, he said.

"Our position is not that medications are bad for you. You may need a combination of a gluten-free diet and drugs," Bitsas said. "If we get them on the proper nutrient-based program, they might be able to reduce the amount of medications they're on."

On his new diet, Dylan may still erupt, but the episodes only last a few minutes and occur much less frequently.

The diet has been a miracle for Dylan and his family, said his grandmother, Emily DeGlopper. Life is much calmer and more pleasant in their home, where Dylan has punched holes in walls, destroyed aluminum siding and smashed a glass oven door during his fits of rage.

"For a while, it was a real bad roller-coaster. You could never know what mood Dyl would be in," said DeGlopper, who has cared for Dylan most of his life. But since he started the gluten-free diet, "it's been a world of difference," she said.

"He's a dream," she said. "It's nicer here."

Dating back to the first grade, Dylan has been charged six times with assault, treated in psychiatric hospitals nearly a dozen times and has alienated his fellow students and neighbors. He's been diagnosed with bipolar disorder and Attention Deficit Hyperactivity Disorder, and also deals with abandonment issues, anxiety and learning disabilities.

At least once a week, Dylan would have a violent outburst, and it would take him hours to calm down. Regular work with an anger-management counselor, therapist and psychiatrist helped, but his explosions were unpredictable and—as he is growing bigger and stronger—dangerous. DeGlopper was afraid another criminal charge would send Dylan to juvenile detention, or that he would seriously injure someone.

On his new diet, Dylan may still erupt, but the episodes only last a few minutes and occur much less frequently, DeGlopper said. Afterward, Dylan realizes what he's done, and is apologetic and cooperative, cleaning up any mess he makes, she said. He's also taking about half the 12 or so daily medications he was on four months [earlier].

Preparing meals with hard-to-find rice flour and potato flour and making sure meats and other foods haven't been tainted with wheat products or MSG can be costly and time-consuming. DeGlopper is trying to shake up the recipes so she's not always feeding Dylan a plain hamburger, cheese and rice.

Moving Forward with Caution

Many mental health practitioners are skeptical of nontraditional therapies, such as acupuncture, reflexology and diet and nutritional treatments. But DeGlopper said she was open to trying nearly anything that could help Dylan.

Dr. Preeti Venkataraman, a Bloomfield Hills, Mich., child and adolescent psychiatrist, said, "It's tough to say" if such alternative treatments are truly effective "because there isn't a lot of data out there backing these things up." She said she doesn't discourage patients from exploring dietary alternatives, but said they should be very cautious about nutritional supplements or herbal remedies, which can interfere with prescription drugs and impact the body.

"When you're treating children you want to be very cautious and careful and go with treatments that have been proven and that have data that's backing up what you're doing," she said.

The diet hasn't been fail-safe. A few weeks ago, Dylan snapped, slamming his fists into a tree and then into the steering wheel of his grandmother's minivan, which he wanted to drive away.

"He wanted me to choke him, put him out of his misery. He explodes, the anger is just horrible," DeGlopper said.

She suspects Dylan—who has learned to carefully read food packaging labels—accidentally ate or drank something containing gluten. This time, though, Dylan's fit didn't last as long, and he let his anger-management counselor help talk him down. Afterward, he apologized, telling his grandmother, "I'm so sorry I could have hurt you."

"There are some days that are harder than others," he said.

Still, while Dylan and his grandmother know they face hurdles, they're committed to him becoming a happy, healthy young man who recognizes what triggers his anger and knows how to deal with it.

"I'm hoping in the long run Dylan's going to do things on his own," DeGlopper said.

Faith Can Turn Anger into a Spiritual Friend

Andrew D. Lester

Andrew D. Lester is professor emeritus of pastoral theology and pastoral counseling at Brite Divinity School, Texas Christian University and the author of several books, including The Angry Christian: A Theology for Care and Counseling.

Are you startled by the suggestion that anger can have a positive role in your life? Anger may feel so dangerous to you that you find it difficult to imagine anger as a *spiritual friend*. If you think of anger as an enemy, or have been exposed to anger that wounds and victimizes, then the idea of anger as a guide on your spiritual pilgrimage may seem ridiculous.

But remember that our capacity for anger is part of being created in the image of God, a gift that has been called "good" and blessed by God. I hope you will invite anger to be a spiritual ally, a partner in striving toward personal wholeness. Many things happen in life that can prevent us from growing and developing into what God would have us to be. We need to be aware of those forces that would keep us immature, dependent, or alienated.

Anger is our ally first and foremost because of its basic function: to warn us of threats to our self. As we have seen, anger arises from the anxiety we feel when our personhood is threatened. It is the early warning system that something is threatening. Anger is an ally when it motivates our defensive and aggressive responses to these threats. It is part of our survival system provided by the Creator.

Anger as a Guide

Anger can also be a spiritual friend when it reveals aspects of our life that we need to work on, correct, and allow to be transformed by the gospel. It is a spiritual ally when we allow it to become a "diagnostic window." By this I mean that if we work to use our anger to understand why we are threatened, we have the opportunity to learn something about ourselves that we might not learn in any other context.

You can use your anger as a spiritual ally in changing the relationship from dependency into one of, first, independence, and then interdependence.

A fever gets our attention because it signals that something is wrong, and we focus quickly on reducing the sick person's temperature. Fevers don't occur, however, unless there is an underlying inflammation, and to treat only the fever, without paying attention to the cause, would be foolish and irresponsible. Likewise, when we're angry we have the responsibility not only to make sure our anger does no harm, but to seek out the underlying threat. Using an experience of anger as a "diagnostic window," and learning what the threats really are, enables us to change our behavior in ways that allow us to love and be loved in new and wonderful ways. Some ways in which anger can be a spiritual ally by aiding us in self-understanding are: recovering our true self, identifying idols, and uncovering guilt and shame.

Recovering Our True Self

We can lose our best self in many ways. Unjust, unfair, or controlling relationships, for example, can cause people to lose their sense of self and their sense of worth. They have been robbed of the spiritual freedom to think, feel, and act in ways that affect the world around them. They feel powerless and helpless, and often accept the "way things are." Instead of being threatened and angry by their powerlessness, they become passive and stay slaves to those who control them. But anger can help us recover our true selves, so that we become the type of person God intended and desires for us. And when that happens, anger can serve some of its most precious roles—defender of the self, protector of self-integrity, and guardian of the self's emotional boundaries.

Daniel's Story

Daniel was twenty-seven years old, single, and in his third year of a graduate program. His major professor sent him to me because he was in danger of flunking out despite his outstanding ability. Daniel came willingly because he was "so depressed all the time" that he couldn't concentrate. He was also worried about what to do after graduation. He would have a master's degree but did not like the jobs available in his field. When I asked why he didn't pursue a job he liked, he said, "Mother would have a fit!"

When we give too much credence to one person's opinion, their approval can become an idol in our lives.

It turned out that Daniel was preparing for a vocation he didn't like because it was the career his mother had planned for him since he was a child. As a dutiful son, he had been pretending interest in this profession, hoping he could learn to like it and satisfy his mother. His mother controlled his behavior in other ways, as well: for instance, he only dated women she approved of because he felt he should marry a person she would like, to keep her happy, and he regularly spent his weekends with his mother. Daniel was trapped in an unhealthy, dependent relationship, trying to choose a vocation and mate based on his mother's approval. . . .

A Modern-Day Slave

Maybe you are wondering whether you have "lost yourself" to another person—spouse, child, boss, or good friend. Perhaps you sometimes feel like a modern-day slave. Ask yourself, Do I feel free to express my thoughts and feelings in this relationship without being rejected or punished? Do I have the freedom to make my own decisions about things important to me? Do I have a vote that counts within the marriage or family situation? Am I respected for my abilities and loyalty at work, recognized as an individual with unique feelings and needs? If the answer to any of these questions is no, then you might want to evaluate whether you can use your anger as a spiritual ally in changing the relationship from dependency into one of, first, independence, and then interdependence.

Anger as Idol Detector

Most Christians are committed to the First Commandment, "You shall have no other gods before me" (Exod. 20:3). Yet we constantly push the Living God from the center of our life and give center stage to the common "stuff" of life as if those things were gods. These "gods" include things such as food, which we eat with little regard for health; money, which we can seek with little awareness of greed; and jobs that can consume us. People such as bosses, children, televangelists, entertainers, and sports figures become gods for some folks. Even ideas such as religious doctrines and political systems become the center of life for some people. In theological language these become idols, inadequate gods. Worship of false gods is subtle, so we often fail to recognize when we have created idols. But just as a metal detector points to hidden metal, anger can help us detect and uncover our idols. . . .

Our relationships can also be idolatrous. When we give too much credence to one person's opinion, their approval can become an idol in our lives, and we live to be pleasing not in God's eyes but in the eyes of a parent, a spouse, or a friend.

Madeline's Story

Madeline was constantly angry when visiting her parents. She and her husband both believed that the anger stemmed from her mother's constant put-downs and criticisms. Her mother was critical of Madeline as a wife, mother, cook, and homemaker, and even of how she dressed. And indeed, much of Madeline's anger was due to her mother's comments.

Things changed when Madeline began to understand her response to her mother. Madeline confessed that she had always been desperate for her mother's approval, which she had never received. Her mother's criticism was a constant threat to the need for her approval. During the process of exploring this anger in the context of her faith, Madeline was able to realize that her desperate need for her mother's approval was a type of "worship." She decided that her mother's opinions had indeed become an idol. We explored the possibility that if she moved God into the position she had heretofore granted to her mother, then perhaps she could trust God's acceptance and love. This idea produced a significant change in Madeline's feelings for herself. She decided to trust the perceptions that her husband, sister, and best friends had of her rather than her mother's critique. Once she had taken her mother out of the idol role, she was also able to accept her mother's "critical personality," as she called it—but it was no longer central in her life. . . .

Sometimes when you ask yourself why you felt threatened, the answer will reveal an idol. Remember that part of dealing with anger creatively is to assess the validity of the threat. It is our Christian responsibility to determine whether those things we're invested in are in sync with our faith or whether they represent our "worship" of values that don't measure up to our faith. Then, as . . . Madeline with her mother, we can choose to push these idols out of the center of our life. We can invite God back into the center. Worship can once again focus on the Living God, who does not need defending. Then we give thanks for anger's role as a spiritual ally.

If the threat is related to guilt, then your faith can guide you through confession, repentance, acceptance of forgiveness, and restitution.

You know how awful it is to realize that you have broken a pledge, hurt someone, cheated, told a lie, acted illegally, or disobeyed your conscience. The guilt and shame can feel so terrible that often we deny or suppress the feeling. It is easy to rationalize guilt by explaining it away, or denying responsibility for what happened, or blaming someone else. Anger propels us on the path toward self-discovery and spiritual growth by allowing us to uncover guilt and shame we might have been denying.

Marilyn and Ken's Story

Marilyn and Ken brought their seventeen-year-old daughter to see me at the counseling center. The daughter had recently told them she was having sexual intercourse with her boyfriend, which made them upset and angry. Their value system about premarital sex had been threatened. They were also afraid that the daughter would get pregnant. Marilyn was so furious that the first session was very difficult, filled mostly with hostile accusations and judgments from the parents, particularly Marilyn. So I cut the session short and scheduled a separate conference for the parents in which we could pursue why Marilyn had so much hostility. Ken finally broke his silence and suggested that Marilyn tell the whole story. She resisted, but finally broke down in tears as she confessed that this daughter, who was sleeping with her boyfriend, had been conceived out of wedlock. . . .

Another reason to be sensitive to your anger and evaluate it carefully is that you might find that the threat represents guilt that you have ignored. When trying to understand a particular incident of anger, you can ask, "Could I be feeling guilty? Is this intense anger related to something I have done, or not done, for which I feel ashamed or embarrassed?" If the threat *is* related to guilt, then your faith can guide you, through confession, repentance, acceptance of forgiveness, and restitution, which allows you to move forward into renewed spiritual vitality. And again you can be thankful for anger as a spiritual friend and guide.

Organizations to Contact

The editors have compiled the following list of organizations concerned with the issues debated in this book. The descriptions are derived from materials provided by the organizations. All have publications or information available for interested readers. The list was compiled on the date of publication of the present volume; the information provided here may change. Be aware that many organizations take several weeks or longer to respond to inquiries, so allow as much time as possible.

American Association of Anger Management Providers (AAAMP)
12301 Wilshire Blvd., Suite 418, Brentwood, CA 90025
(310) 207-3591
e-mail: georgeanderson@aol.com
Web site: www.aaamp.org

The American Association of Anger Management Providers has been formed to address the interests of anger management service providers. The AAAMP offer its members professional development through state and national conferences, study groups, and networking opportunities. Articles published by the AAAMP include, *Look Back at Anger* and *Healthy Anger Management: A Proactive Emphasis.*

American Psychiatric Association (APA)
1000 Wilson Blvd., Suite 1825, Arlington, VA 22209-3901
(703) 907-7300
Web site: www.psych.org

The American Psychiatric Association is an organization of psychiatrists working together to ensure humane care and effective treatment for all persons with mental disorders. The APA vision is a society that has available accessible quality psychiatric diagnosis and treatment. APA is the publisher of the *Diagnostic and Statistical Manual of Mental Disorders,* the *American Journal of Psychiatry, Psychiatric News,* and other leading journals as well as more than seven hundred books in print.

American Psychological Association (APA)
750 First St. NE, Washington, DC   20002-4242
(800) 374-2727
Web site: www.apa.org

The American Psychological Association is the largest organization in the United States representing the field of psychology and the world's largest association of psychologists. Founded in 1892, APA is dedicated to advancing psychology as a science, as a profession, and as a means of promoting human welfare. The official journal of the APA, *American Psychologist* is the authoritative source for substantive and feature articles advancing the field of psychology.

British Association of Anger and Stress Management (BAAM)
East Brinstead, West Sussex
   United Kingdom
+44 (0)845 1300 286
e-mail: info@angermanage.co.uk
Web site: www.angermanage.co.uk

The British Association of Anger Management is focused on all aspects of anger and conflict management. BAAM offers support, programs, and training for the general public, children and teenagers, government bodies, corporations, the educational sector, personnel/HR management, trainers, counselors, and anyone dealing with their own or another's anger.

National Association for Cognitive-Behavioral Therapists (NACBT)
PO Box 2195, Weirton, WV   26062
(800) 853-1135 • fax: (304) 723-3982
Web site: www.nacbt.org

The National Association of Cognitive-Behavioral Therapists is an organization dedicated solely to the teaching and practice of cognitive-behavioral psychotherapy. The NACBT is the leading organization dedicated exclusively to supporting, promoting, teaching, and developing cognitive-behavioral therapy and those who practice it. NACBT publications include *The Client's Guide to Cognitive-Behavioral Therapy, You and Your Emotions, Rational Living Therapy Level-One Certification Home Study Program*, and *Help Yourself to Happiness*.

National Institute of Mental Health (NIMH)

6001 Executive Blvd. Rm. 8184, MSC 9663
Bethesda, MD   20892-9663
(866) 615-6464
e-mail: nimhinfo@nih.gov
Web site: www.nimh.nih.gov

The National Institute of Mental Health is the largest scientific organization in the world dedicated to research focused on the understanding, treatment, and prevention of mental disorders and the promotion of mental health. NIMH's mission is to reduce the burden of mental illness and behavioral disorders through research on the mind, brain, and behavior.

Office on Violence Against Women (OVW)

U.S. Department of Justice, Washington, DC   20530-0001
(202) 514-2000
e-mail: askdoj@usdoj.gov
Web site: www.ovw.usdoj.gov

The mission of the Office on Violence Against Women is to provide federal leadership to reduce violence against women and to administer justice for and strengthen services to all victims of domestic violence, dating violence, sexual assault, and stalking. This is accomplished by developing and supporting the capacity of state, local, tribal, and nonprofit entities involved in responding to violence against women. The OVW has numerous publications available on its Web site.

Society of Human Resource Management (SHRM)
1800 Duke St., Alexandria, VA   22314
(800) 283-7476
Web site: www.shrm.org

The Society for Human Resource Management is the world's largest professional association devoted to human resource (HR) management. The society's mission is to serve the needs of HR professionals by providing the most current and comprehensive resources, and to advance the profession by promoting HR's essential, strategic role. SHRM publications include, *HR Magazine, HR Week, Managing Smart, Mosaics, Echoes Student Newsletter*, and *Workplace Visions.*

Bibliography

Books

Rhoda Baruch, Suzanne Stutman, and Edith H. Grotberg | *Creative Anger: Putting That Powerful Emotion to Good Use.* Westport, CT: Greenwood, 2007.

Diane M. Berry and Terry J. Berry | *Peace of My Mind: A Therapist's Guide to Handling Anger and Other Difficult Emotions.* Manitowoc, WI: Blue Waters, 2008.

John E. Bradshaw | *When Madness Is Sane.* Houston: John Bradshaw Media Group, 2008.

Kate Collins-Donnelly | *Starving the Anger Gremlin: Anger Management for Young People.* Victoria, BC: Trafford, 2007.

William Davies | *Overcoming Anger and Irritability: A Self-Help Guide Using Cognitive Behavioral Techniques.* New York: Basic Books, 2008.

Georg H. Eifert, Matthew McKay, John P. Forsyth, and Steven C. Hayes | *Act on Life Not on Anger: The New Acceptance and Commitment Therapy Guide to Problem Anger.* Oakland, CA: New Harbinger, 2006.

Susan Gingras Fitzell | *Transforming Anger to Personal Power: An Anger Management Curriculum for Grades 6–12.* Champaign, IL: Research Press, 2007.

Mike George   *Don't Get Mad Get Wise: Why No One Ever Makes You Angry . . . Ever!* Berkeley, CA: O Books, 2007.

Ida Greene   *Anger Management: Skills for Children; Teens.* London: People Skills International, 2008.

Mary Ellen Halloran   *Anger: Let the Tiger Out, but Keep It On a Leash.* Oakland, CA: Timepiece, 2007.

Ruth King   *Healing Rage: Women Making Inner Peace Possible.* New York: Penguin, 2008.

David MacQuarrie   *Blowing Out the Darkness: The Management of Emotional Life Issues Especially Anger and Rage.* Bloomington, IN: Authorhouse, 2008.

Gladeana McMahon   *No More Anger.* London: Karnac, 2008.

Tim Murphy and Loriann H. Oberlin   *Overcoming Passive-Aggression: How to Stop Hidden Anger from Spoiling Your Relationships, Career and Happiness.* New York: Barnes & Noble, 2007.

Kathleen O'Bannon   *Anger Cure: A Step-by-Step Program to Reduce Anger, Rage, Negativity, Violence, and Depression in Your Life.* Laguna Beach, CA: Basic Health, 2007.

Calvin Sandborn   *Becoming the Kind Father: A Son's Journey.* Gabriola Island, BC: New Society, 2007.

Leonard Scheff   *The Cow in the Parking Lot: A Guide for Transforming Anger for a Happier, More Effective Life.* Lincoln, NE: iUniverse, 2008.

Brenda Shoshanna   *The Anger Diet: Thirty Days to Stress-Free Living.* Kansas City, MO: Andrews McMeel, 2005.

Karen D. Wasoba   *Lord, Shut Me Up! Anger Management for Christian Women.* Tucson, AZ: Wheatmark, 2007.

Periodicals

Jacqui Brewster and Ada Montgomery   "Stop Winding Me Up," *Learning Disability Practice*, May 2005.

Maria Cramer   "Fewer Batterers Put into Programs; Victims' Advocates Fault Plea Bargains," *Boston Globe*, April 8, 2008.

Mike Davies   "Film Style: Mad for It; Road Rage, Plane Rage, and Technological Tantrums," *Birmingham Post* (UK), June 4, 2003.

Maureen Freely et al.   "Why Are Women Always Seeing Red?" *Sunday Times* (London), January 6, 2008.

Kevin Hoffman, Heather Loeb, and Kyle Western   "Why So Angry?" *Men's Health*, May 2007.

Ziba Kashef   "Is Your Temper over the Top?" *Health*, October 2006.

Annie Kelly "Prickly Subject: People Who Are Violent Can Change, According to One Charity That Refuses to Disguise Its Work as 'Anger Management' and Has Helped Hundreds of Men and Women to Stop Lashing Out at Others," *Guardian* (Manchester, UK), January 2, 2008.

Ronald Kotulak "Explosive Rage Not as Rare as Once Thought, Study Finds," *Chicago Tribune*, June 5, 2006.

Matthai Kuruvila "Freedom from Anger," *San Francisco Chronicle*, March 23, 2008.

Jim Larson "Angry and Aggressive Students," *Education Digest*, March 2008.

Dominic Lawson "The Progressive Case for Imprisonment," *Independent* (London), November 20, 2007.

Katherine Liepe-Levinson "Anger Management Using the Actor's Skills and General Semantics," *ETC: A Review of General Semantics*, April 1, 2006.

Andy Meisler "The Storm's Quiet Eye; How Cool, Calm and Emotionally Brilliant Brentwood Psychotherapist-Entrepreneur George Anderson Built an Empire from L.A.'s Limitless Supply of Hotheads," *Los Angeles Times*, August 28, 2005.

Martin Miller   "Anger Management All the Rage,
                       but Does It Help?" *Los Angeles Times*,
                       February 8, 2004.

Michael Craig   "Violence as a Medical Issue," *Har-*
Miller   *vard Mental Health Letter*, October
                       2006.

Nate Poppino   "The Journey Home: Iraq Troops
                       Find Resources to Ease Transition,"
                       Tribune Business News, November 11,
                       2007.

Mark Porter   "Control Yourself," *Evening Standard*
                       (London), March 25, 2008.

S. Ramachander   "Board Rage," *Businessline*, February
                       11, 2008.

Tim Rayment   "The Age of Rage," *Sunday Times*
                       (London), July 16, 2006.

Cheryl   "Getting Smart About Getting Mad:
Richardson   Anger Can Be a Messenger and a
                       Motivator," *Good Housekeeping*, April
                       2003.

Abigail Wild   "When the Red Mist Descends; Is It
                       All Getting Out of Control?" *Herald*
                       (Glasgow, Scotland), June 6, 2003.

Index